SO-ASL-817

Directions in Life

for the

Occasionally

Confused

J. J. Elliott, MA, MFT

John F. Elliott, MA. MFT.

PUBLISH
AMERICA

PublishAmerica

Baltimore

First printing

ISBN: 1-4137-3438-3
PUBLISHED BY PUBLISHAMERICA, LLLP
www.publishamerica.com
Baltimore

Printed in the United States of America

What They Say About John Foster Elliot

Scott Miller, PhD, author of *The Heart and Soul of Change*, states, "John Elliott tells stories with the depth of Socrates, the insight of a Zen Master and the wit of Dave Berry."

Gary Cooper, LCSW, contributing editor of the Psychotherapy Networker, states, "John Elliott is that rare combination of an intelligent, philosophical, humorous and empathic therapist...a paragon of paradox, an idol of irony and a hunter of the heart."

Barry Duncan, PhD, founder of the Institute for the Study of Therapeutic Change, states, "John Elliott inspires us with his lyrical prose to not only challenge our most cherished beliefs but also attain that most sought after but rarely achieved harmony in our lives."

Acknowledgements

Although writing can be a solitary task, no one really accomplishes much alone. However tall we may appear, it's only because we are standing on the the achievements of others before us and around us. This book is dedicated to my wife Beth, my best friend, true love and partner for life. Without her I may have had no direction at all.

Many thanks to all of my supporters and teachers: David Gottlieb, Richard Snyder, Ron Murphy, Guy Pilato, Marty Marder, Barbara Walkshul and the O.D. staff and volunteers at Penn State, Wilson "Skip" Smith, Eric Marcus, Melvin Suhd, Warren Dohemann, Irma Stranz, Ev Arronberg, Scott Miller, Barry Duncan, Gary Cooper, Jim Walt, Deborah Harper, John Riolo, John Summers, Vicke Ficht and the Sunrise crew, Jack, Sandy, David, Josh, Jon, Angie, and Cole Kesselman, Jerry Paul, Chris and Angie Phillips, Mike Blum and Titan Recording, Tom Trimble, Dick at Awe-Struck, Jean Cox, Vic, Ruth, Vic JR, Margie, Rachel, Katie, Becky, Mark and Shari, Mike, Chris, Lisa and Jim Elliott, the Wards, the McCauges, Peg Foster, my grandfather and namesake, John R. Foster and almost last but not least PublishAmerica and my competent and capable editor Cat McAteer.

Finally, I wish to acknowledge all my clients and countless others who have touched my heart, inspired my mind and enriched my soul.

Contents

SO...
Want to GROW?
You want to CHANGE?
You want to learn to be FULLY ALIVE? GOOD.
Maybe that's why you chose this book.

But there IS a price to pay, and it's not just the money
you paid to read this.
Or maybe you just liked the title.
– Could be a great gift for...somebody else – right?

Remember one thing even if you forget all the other
stuff you learn here:
You are worth the investment.
There is only one of you in this entire universe.
This makes you rare and valuable.
Remember this.

Sometimes we need directions about how to read directions. On a road map, this is often called the "key."

Chapter 1: Learning How to Learn

This is a book that will help get you to some meanings in life. Some directions you'll read are pretty clear cut and easy to follow. Other guidance here may seem obscure and vague. Understanding can't always be achieved through a straight line. Most of us attempt to reduce meaning into one static concept or belief. If you take one still frame from a motion picture it's not the same as seeing the entire film.

That's just what we do with words and communication.

Life is more than making the point, finding the bottom line and going around in circles. Any journey about meaning can't simply be about the destination.

How we travel is a trip in itself.

If we're really going to understand, we need to know in ways that add movement, depth and possibility to our lives. We need to learn how to make choices just as much as we need to learn what choices to make.

A story, a metaphor or a fable may convey us to those deeper meanings.

For the last twenty-five years I've been a psychotherapist in Los Angeles California. (Yeah, it's a great place for a shrink – lots of work).

My other job, like yours, is to live the rest of my life. I struggle with the same issues as most people who come to see me.

Like how to care for others without being uncaring to myself – How to allow someone to love me without screwing it up. And how and when to confront someone who takes advantage of me, and figuring out why the hell I let them in the first place.

You know the problems. We all have the same ones. They come from being human.

So, I began to write both for myself and for my clients. I looked through other sciences and disciplines for new ways of thinking about things. I searched through my own field of psychology and many others. What I came up with was this book you are reading. I didn't come up with the One Answer, or The Way, or How to Be Completely and Absolutely Successful, Powerful and Happy and Find Your Perfect Mate As You Lose Twenty Pounds Making Everybody Love You Course of Miracles Prophecy Happily Ever After Conversations with God Book. (Although I have considered the title).

The only thing that we can ever be certain of is change. The universe is always changing.

And this scares the crap out of most of us.

We act like drowning swimmers grasping on to any illusion of stability, hanging on for dear life. But no one can stop this movement. Maybe because we are so powerless we try to grab on to anything that resembles certainty. We do this by making *one thing our everything, always.*

The pain can be our everything – or even the joy. It could be money, or sex, or food. But it's always just *one* belief, – *one* love, *one* reason...*one* answer.

We make the One Thing mean so much that no meaning is left for anything else. The myths abound from ancient cultures that when you honored only one god, the rest of the gods would kick your ass. We all want the Midas touch – and when we get it and everything turns to gold...

Then of course we can't eat because the food is gold, we can't sleep because the bed is gold, and we can't touch those we love...

One problem with self-help books is that we make up these general rules of living, when life itself is composed of specific events. We tell you what to do and help you rob yourself of your free will and right to make choices. We end up asking ridiculous questions, such as – is it better to be open or to be closed?

Well, is it better to have diarrhea or to be constipated?

It all depends. In general, all answers depend on the specific situation. At one instant of time, our one Thing may be the most important thing in the universe to get and hold on to. At the next moment, we had better learn to be able to give it up and let go so we can deal with what comes next. Everything we know and have will eventually change. Like waves coming in from the ocean, change is a continual force that gently washes over us, or throws us tumbling into the sand.

Our basic dilemma involves preserving the essence of ourselves, of what we value as noble and good while changing other aspects of self in order to survive. And – of knowing when to take a stand and work instead to change the world around us and "To be – AND not to be" really is the answer. Although what we "have" will change, what we "are" may be our only point of certainty in a most uncertain world.

It's not just a matter of learning to surrender or fight. At separate times each may be appropriate. We have to learn to value both, and add them together to make something completely different. I believe that our solutions rest in simple things we do in everyday life. If we have learned to do these things in one place, we can learn to do them in other areas as well. That's what we're going to explore in these pages. Guidelines for the journey we call life. Points of Direction for the occasionally confused. That's you. And me. And all of us. We're all in this together.

Whenever you're getting guidance, there's always a few things to bear in mind...

Guidelines for Using Guidelines

1. Guidelines are simply maps that help us find direction in our lives. Most guides are useful, providing that they do not obstruct our vision of the road or our capability to steer, brake and shift gears along the way.

2. For this reason, all travelers who have the compulsive desire to be able to see everything and know it all are warned against taping these instructions to their windshields or glasses. Although it is important to know where you can go, it is equally important to be able to see what's really *present* around you. All guidelines, rules, and maps should be kept to the side when one is in motion. Do not hold on to them; just keep them within reach.

3. If used long enough, most guidelines can turn into rulers. Straight lines may be the shortest distance between two points, but aren't always the best way to get there from here. A ruler is a tool for measurement, and should not become a petty tyrant that dictates your behavior. (After all, if your map says go over the bridge, and

your bridge is washed out, are you just going to drive over the cliff?) The map, ruler, or guideline should not be confused with the territory.

4. When entering new and unfamiliar lands, it may be useful to borrow a map from a friend you respect and trust. If there are no guidelines available, begin to make up your own. Do this by observing prior to taking any immediate action. Otherwise you're driving blind.

5. Your old maps of other territories were the best you could come up with at one time. There still may be great value to them. See if they are applicable.

6. There is an exception to every guideline and rule that you make or find. Guidelines are always works-in-progress because even if they are completed, the territory they describe is forever changing. With this in mind, make sure that your guidelines have ample space for corrections and change.

7. Although imitation is the sincerest form of flattery, we must ask ourselves at times, "Flattering to whom?"

All of these guidelines in this book were written for John F. Elliott. You can borrow any and all of them for your own use.

However, the "one size fits all" approach has been known to create uncomfortable fits. You may end up with material that chokes you with restricted limitations, or trips you with unnecessary excess. The author strongly advises you to suit yourself by fashioning your own Guidelines.

Here's another way to look at using advice... from anyone. Mine too.

Rulers and Maps

When I was just a kid, I could never draw a straight line. So I used a ruler. A ruler is really just this little stick we use to measure space. With the ruler you could say that I had a "guide" line. Eventually, some of us learn to draw fairly straight lines without their assistance. Of course, that's just one kind of ruler. Another kind is the king, queen, president, pope, you-name-it type of authority. These rulers draw the lines all by themselves.

Inside of all of us, well, I believe that we still carry rulers. These help us to be straight, (or gay, depending on your biological imperative). Rulers provide continuity, associating one point to another, and give us something to measure ourselves by – Or the ruler can rigidly dictate our path of action.

We call these rulers "values," or "principles." When you give your word to yourself, and/or someone else about a future action or even about a past one, you are defining yourself. In a way, you are drawing yourself and them a map of who you are for wherever and whenever. The difficulty arises in how we are use the map. If we let it dictate to us, period, then, we certainly can feel secure in knowing that we always know the way. So the map says we cross the bridge there to get to our destination.

But when there becomes here, and we see that the bridge is washed out, well, some of us drive straight off the cliff. Our ruler was in command.

Perhaps we need to remember that the ruler, value or principle is actually just a hired guide or elected help. You see – no matter how well we think we know the lay of the land, it's always changing. And there are always those areas that have never been mapped. So we don't know always. We can only know sometimes. We don't have to throw the map away. It's still useful. We also don't have to tape it across our windshield so that it obstructs our vision. We do this at times, and then think we can see everything. So we drive off with the map completely blocking our view, get into accidents, and blame it on the map. Then we try to get a "better" map, and tape that one up next. Perhaps it's best to keep all maps to one side and consult them when we are feeling lost. Perhaps it might be good to have enough room on them to be able to chart new territories found only when we use our common senses.

Attitudes are a blend of feelings and beliefs. To have to be "right" serves us well in do or die situations. However, developing a "right attitude" requires more than mere desire. If we are only allowed to take right turns we end up going in circles. Both left and right are necessary for direction.

The Left Attitude

The left attitude thinks and feels with all the colors and grays. The left attitude ignores itself. We're not trying to be right. It's just a by-product, a pleasant friction of movement that is a flowing without haste. A left attitude manifests an abundance of time, as it grows outside of seasons and schedules.

A left attitude is forged in process and tempered by results. A left attitude recognizes perfection in doing one's best, as opposed to being the best.

A left attitude doesn't oppose being the best either. "Being" the best – it's just another offshoot. We can never *have* the left attitude. We can only be the left attitude.

The Right Attitude

The right attitude knows absolutely that there is only black and white.

There is only room for certainty. A right attitude is forged in results and tempered by process. A right attitude must be the best and win, or lose itself. There are no by-products and everything is for a reason. Even if it's the reason we are making up.

We can always have the right attitude. Even when we're wrong.

In general, the left attitude helps us to be free, the right attitude helps us to be secure. Take your pick.

Guidelines for Influencing Beliefs and Attitudes

1. All beliefs and attitudes are worthy of respect, if only for the

power they have to influence behavior.

2. Our respect should be given regardless of the content of such declarations. We respect all beliefs and attitudes as reflections of the human need for security and freedom. Respecting should be discriminated from approval or support here.

3. Attempts to denigrate and belittle or forcibly remove most beliefs and attitudes will only create resistance. Attempting to convince another by negating their perceptions and understanding creates defensiveness and opposition.

4. However, most convictions may be transformed, provided that:
   a)   Their underlying intent is validated
   b)   An alternate empowering belief or attitude is available
   c)   The individual is open to change

5. The individuals perception of the change agent defines that person to be empathic and genuine in their concern and knowledgeable regarding content. Most of us just want to feel secure, or free, or loved and may lack the means to accomplish this.

6. Even negative and self-destructive thoughts have protective and proactive elements to them. They may help one to avoid or control anticipated pain and loss as well as setting up another to have control and power.

7. Other influences to attitudes and beliefs may be the unconscious, the family, peers, culture, society, biochemistry, situations, or some other higher order/process we lack the capability to intellectually comprehend.

8. We must be open to include these other systems in our considerations when we wish to influence change. Our personal tools

here will be our intellect, imagination, affect, and sensory process.

9. Integrity, compassion, humor and creativity need to be included in every system of belief.

Life is the one classroom that's always in session. All of us will be learning for the rest of our lives. When we stop, we're dead, – physically, emotionally, intellectually or spiritually. Once you learn how to learn, then anything may be possible...

The Best Teacher

The best teacher depends on what and when you need to learn.

I have not found books on "How To Swim" very useful for the drowning person. (Nor do they give the beginner much confidence either).

There are some things only learned through experience.

At the same time, it really tics me off when I have been playing guitar for thirty years, and some young rocker playing for six months blows me away.

Experience is not always a guarantee.

There are some talents that are gifts. Some of us lucked out in the mechanical department, or the academic department, or in the artistic department, or in the advanced class of charm, or athletics. We all have stuff we are naturally good at, and we all have things to learn.

If we add the Total You up, you would always equal the Total Me.

I know it doesn't always feel that way. You might be actively searching to see who is better or worse. Well, some people are better in a specific way, in a specific place, at a specific time. No doubt. You don't know everything about them, or even about yourself for that matter. We are like diamonds. One facet of the diamond may be beautiful; it is all the facets together which give the stone its worth. A diamond never knows its own value.

Taking in knowledge and learning how to use what you've learned are two different processes.

You can eat a lot of food, but if the food remains undigested, there wasn't much point to the meal.

So, if you wish to learn something new, it might be advisable to bear a few things in mind.

1) *It's hard to eat on a full stomach.*

If you are already certain that you know all about what you are going to learn, your mind is full (possibly "full of it"). In this case, don't partake. I'm sure that you will spend most of your time bellyaching instead of paying attention. Don't waste time for you and the teacher.

2) *Eating too much on an empty stomach is dangerous.*

If it's been some time since your thirst for knowledge has been quenched, don't drown yourself. You'll only puke all of it up. Start with something light and simple.

3) *Take small bites and chew them over.*

Large bites that go unchewed have two undesirable results. These involve choking and indigestion. You can only take so much in at once. We need to break information down so that it's easily swallowed. If you do manage to cram it all in, don't expect to be able to put it to good use. Unfortunately, when we learn in this way, we maintain a bad taste for whatever was dished out.

4) *Select a diet that has some variety.*

You may have a main course of knowledge that you pursue. Eating the same fare day after day can be very unrewarding, and may even be a health hazard. We take in foods that provide certain amounts of protein, amino acids, vitamins, minerals, and fiber. Specializing in a particular area of knowledge is like just eating chicken seven days a week.

Throw in some potatoes, vegetables, fruits and dessert. You will feel more "balanced." Trust me on this one.

5) *No matter how good the meal is, there will always be some residue that needs to be eliminated.*
Not everything you learn is going to fit with you. Some of it shouldn't. It's just there to help you bind other information that is useless to you personally. Find some garden and use it for fertilizer.

6) *No matter how bad the meal is, there will always be some portion that needs to be swallowed.*
Perhaps you have learned that you have a bad teacher. Use the learning to drop out of the class. On the other hand, many tastes are acquired. We grow to like things. Even fish eggs, sour grapes, and cheese with mold.

Stay with the meal long enough to really see if the taste might have some merit. If you know it's going to give you heartburn or nausea, select a different menu. Many times the food may be of the highest quality. You just happened to find a lousy cook. At other times, the food may be of poor quality, but the chef has these excellent sauces. Learn to tell the difference. That's for all of you Learners out there.

I have something else for the Teachers.
The very first thing a Teacher must do is Learn. You must be a student of your students. You must learn about your students, and discover what they already know. Find out if your student really wants to take the class, and what they want to learn. (If I'm not really qualified to teach in this area, I always send them to a Teacher who is).
I first discover the skills and capabilities of those that wish to learn. I usually teach people with what they know already. All the stuff your students already know is one big THIS. Then I can show how THIS is also really like THAT. "THAT" is the new stuff I'm going to teach. For example, how eating is like learning. Of course, there is one major drawback: when people don't have THIS to start with. Perhaps they immigrated from Biafra, or Ethiopia, or some

urban or rural starvation zone.

So in this case you have to Provide An Experience. The experience of being fed and of being hungry if they're overweight. The experience of being held and of being held accountable. The experiences of gratification and frustration. As gratification is the mother to the child, frustration is the father to the adult. When a child begins to stand on their own two feet, mothering and fathering are both beneficial.

I was working with a woman a while ago. We were attempting to "teach" her how to become more assertive. Her husband physically abused her. For the life of me, I couldn't get her to take a stand on this. She wouldn't leave him, and she wouldn't report him to the authorities. For six months we did all of the practicing in the world, and she was the most obedient aggressive client I could ever ask for. But she still wouldn't assert on her own. I had to order her to. And in this, I became just like her controlling husband. So, I had to Provide An Experience.

I'd like to say that I did this On Purpose. I didn't. I forgot about her appointment one week. Really forgot. And scheduled someone else in her place. There I was, doing my best to connect with this new client, being thoughtful and empathic. Ten minutes into the session, my door bursts open.

You should have seen her. She let me have it up and down, left and right. I stood there and took it, because it was well deserved. She was magnificently assertive. I was stupendously submissive. My new client was a bit upset…After she stormed out of my office she left her old man.

In this, two things were Taught and Learned. She could be angry at a Teacher she cared for without having to drop the class. She learned that I have my failings as well. I learned (again) that I don't have to be perfect or in control in order to influence change.

The Best Teacher depends on what you need.

If the Truth is "out there" then we better be prepared to go out there far enough to find it.

Guidelines About the Truth

1. The only truth you can ever be certain of is about yourself, and even here leave room for occasional doubt.

2. What you think to be true about any situation will be as accurate as any good map. The territory isn't always going to stay like your picture.

3. If "Everything is bullshit," this statement is as much a part of that bullshit as anything else. If everything is meaningless, so is this very statement that "everything is meaningless."

4. There is one sure way you can always tell the truth to whomever is pestering or nagging you. Simply state: "I don't think this is any of your business," and inform them that further interrogation is only likely to provide the opportunity for deceit.

5. The truth of a feeling is always more powerful than the truth of a thought in the short run. In the long run, the thoughts will rewrite the history that the heart has made.

6. If there are any absolute truths, they will exist despite what we feel, despite what we think, and despite what we sense.

7. One small truth to hold on to is that everybody makes the best possible choice that they can to take care of what is most important to them. (Even when they don't know it).

8. The truth is, our reactions have very little to do with choice until we become aware we are reacting.

9. The only human quality more powerful than belief is faith. Belief grows from our intellect and senses while faith is nurtured from our hearts and imagination. These days it appears we have much to believe, and so very little in which to invest our faith.

Remember that appearances are deceptive.

10. A truth I've found is at least fifty percent of all activity should be pointless. Happiness does not have a point or angle; it has curves, softness, and a sense of the absurd.

Our minds need to be fed so we can continue to grow. How we take in information does have an effect...

Food for Thoughts

I enjoy steak, a baked potato with everything, a salad with bleu cheese dressing, some vegetables, and a cold beverage. Followed by coffee, and a piece of chocolate cake with vanilla ice cream.

Sound good?

Now, get a large bowl or blender. Throw in the steak, potato, salad, dressing, veggies, coffee, ice cream and cake. Mix well and eat it.

I don't think so.

Imagine that you need to take something inside of you. It could be this meal, or maybe food for thought, or for feelings, or for the senses, or even the imagination. Even if we can mix whatever it is together, if we try to swallow all of it at once we will choke. You can take in all of the smells, and all of the sounds, and all of sights. All at once. Which is okay. That's how I meditate.

Unless you try to make them into one thing. Just one meaning. If you do this, you may miss the varied and subtle tastes of life. We eat to satisfy some need, some hunger. We also eat to enjoy the process of tasting. Hopefully, you can be hungry enough to enjoy every bite. To insure proper digestion, take one mouthful at a time, taste it, chew it carefully, and then swallow. Food for thought should not be gulped. It only causes indigestion.

INTRODUCTION QUESTIONS

1) What do you want to change about your feelings and thoughts regarding yourself?

2) Towards others?

3) What do you think will be necessary to make this change occur? (don't be a smartass and include hell freezing over)

4) When you do change, how will you think, feel and act differently?

5) How will others respond differently?

6) When's the last time you did something nice, relaxing and enjoyable for yourself or somebody else? (You know, you could stop answering these stupid questions and get off your ass and do number 6 right now).

The FOUNDATION of our SECURITY
is built upon CONSISTENCY.

It's what TRUST is all about.

When we trust others or ourselves to fail it's not
because we enjoy suffering and misery...
– it's based on our past disappointments.

At times, we all desire stability.

But the only constant in some of our lives is LOSS.
Some of us do our damnedest to keep it the one thing
we can count on.

Here are some ways to CHANGE...

~~~~~~

Chapter 2: Hope and Trust

Once trust and hope have died in us, resurrecting them is no easy task.

It may be easier for us to give up than to become disappointed in others and ourselves again. We learn from an early age what to receive from this world, and the classes we attend can be filled with abuse, neglect, and disappointment. They also may be filled with false praise and indulgence, leaving us feeling superior even as we continue to score miserably in the tests of life. This chapter is about dealing with loss and grief. The guides and stories here all relate to the ways we have learned to deal with emotional pain. Accepting our vulnerabilities is one part of this process. Another aspect is learning how to receive love and nurturing from others without becoming weaker. Some of us learn to swallow everything; some learn to spit out anything that's offered to them. In either case, the one thing that's missing is the right to make a choice. In our culture, to be called "dependent" is often a put-down for being weak and helpless. As we are all dependent on food, air, and the department of water and power to survive, it's quite ironic that when we deny ourselves these "dependencies," we end up sick or dead. At times, we must depend on ourselves, no doubts about it. However, perhaps our greatest weakness as Americans is the refusal to make cooperation as important as our need for individuality. Here you will learn about the purpose of solitude, the strength of vulnerability, the secret victories hidden behind self-defeating behavior, and about how we keep faith and hope alive by blaming ourselves. You'll also learn how to change certain patterns of thinking, and how and why we do need to experience certain kinds of pain.

Depression is not just an illness, it's also part of a cure...

Darkrooms and Sunburn

You have heard the old saying, "If you fall off a horse, the best thing to do is get right back on." However, if you have splintered and broken bones, it can be a very dangerous thing to do. If you have severe sunburn, nobody says that you should "get right back out into that sun." (Except perhaps, the leading suntan lotion manufacturers). You can go back into the sun if you have sufficient protection.

So, quite simply, if you have been burned, and you keep getting burned, and you don't know what's burned you...

Stay in the dark until you've figured it out.

Depression is not always an illness. It's a way of adjusting to significant losses. Whether it's someone you love, or a job or a home, you've lost them and the future you had planned. Right now, there may be nothing that will or even should make you feel better. You're in pain and grieving. That's where most photographers develop pictures – both old and new. In a darkroom.

We learn unconsciously that it is profitable to be helpless. Unfortunately, it's fool's gold most of the time.

Victory of Defeat

He toddled into the kitchen, thirsty for water and attention. Mom was busy at the oven, cooking and stirring as good moms often do. Dad was on the couch, finally taking some time to himself after being the hard worker he was. There were no villains.

He asked in a nice way, as he had been taught to be polite. "Cin I hab sum wah wah, pweese?" Both parents were preoccupied, and they couldn't give him the attention he requested. He tugged at them again and was further rebuked. Dinner would be soon, they said. Just wait.

Waiting for children is placing them in Purgatory. We forget that time is different for a child. To a three-year-old, ten minutes might equal an hour or two of adult time. (Hey, when you're one day old, that day is your whole life. When you're forty, that one day is one of the 14,600 days you've had so far). Besides, he was still thirsty. So he began to pull out the drawers. He would make his own stairway to the glass beyond his reach. He got up the one, and crawled onto the counter. It was a struggle but he made it. He was BIG now. Just as he reached the cupboard, and pulled it open, the force of his pull threw him off balance.

He fell crashing to the floor, smashing his head. He screamed in fear and pain. Then they came. At first they were gentle and soothing and cooing with sweet shushes and there there's. It will be all right now, they said. Of course, when they discovered his injuries were minor, they yelled at him for being so stupid as to attempt to do things for himself.

Then they got him that glass of water. So he learned that he would be ignored if he chose to ask for help. Asking for help just made him more helpless. (Later in life he would ask the incapable ones, or he would manage to find the one moment when the other was too busy or too tired).

So he learned that if he initiated things on his own, he would fall and be hurt. Doing things for and by yourself guaranteed failure. (Later in life he would only initiate tasks beyond his reach. He would step on or pull on people until he got knocked down. The efforts he made here shocked those who thought him lazy. He never really was).

When he was knocked down, smashed and beaten, there was always someone who came to him with a tall cool glass of water. And he never had to ask. And he never had to get it for himself.

The victory of defeat.

Pain is not quite the enemy we'd like to believe.

Necessary Suffering

There is a certain value to pain. It lets us know we're injured. It helps us to heal, as we are forced to handle those injured parts with care and attention. We may have to give up certain activities and responsibilities until we are well enough. Otherwise, we get hurt even more, and we may be ineffective in the tasks we have chosen to undertake. Pain can allow us to reach out to others for help as well.

Unless, of course, you are a leper. People stay away from lepers. They are afraid they will catch it.

You know, it's that biblical disease. The one where your body begins to rot and fall apart. Noses and fingers turning black with gangrene and smell of death. Most people don't know what leprosy really is. It is a skin disease that produces a condition of neuro-anesthesia. Anesthesia meaning lepers don't feel pain. Consequently, when lepers are injured, they don't always know it. Wounds, cuts, and sprains are often ignored. The body, in turn, continues to deteriorate and decay. Because there is no pain. In order to fully take care of themselves, lepers must scan their bodies in mirrors so they can detect injury. They might do this several times per day.

Often, when we attempt to make someone or ourselves feel "better," we are trying to take that pain away. Pain can be removed artificially due to the wonders of modern medicine. This may be necessary when we have major surgery or terminal illness. Taking away pain prematurely, however, can mask dangerous symptoms and actually jeopardize the healing process. We can help create that condition of leprosy in others, even with the best intentions: Don't feel sad, don't feel bad, don't feel guilty, don't feel angry, don't feel…

Then of course, when the condition of leprosy has taken root, we can shun them, because they will have transformed into unfeeling bitch/bastards. The most important thing we can do for people at times is to let them know that we see what they feel. Even for the lepers. To let them know what they could be feeling. A warm mirror that stays to reflect the unfelt. It's called acceptance.

The cure for leprosy is necessary suffering. You see, it isn't feeling for a friend that matters so much. It's being able to feel with them.

So, next time – when a a friend is in pain…Don't try to fix them – they aren't broken. Before you give them the twenty-five sure-fire solutions for getting "better" – acknowledge their right to feel bad.

Not every thought you think is "you." Your real thoughts are the ones you construct for yourself. Here is one way to deal with uninvited ideas and negative thinking.

Guidelines for Changing Self-Condemnation

1. Give up the belief that you are making these thoughts happen. Most intrusive thoughts are uninvited echoes from past experiences. Others are reflections of biological urges (like sexuality and

aggression) that we have a difficult time accepting as normal. You could be punishing yourself over some past guilt. Some may be indicative of a biochemical imbalance that can effect our thinking. (Chances are that if you have really put forth an effort in attempting to deal with this stuff in the past, then you fall into the last category).

2. If these thoughts are cutting and putting you down, putting yourself down for having them just adds insult to injury. Here you are creating more echoes that condemn you. (I know this for a fact as it's gotten pretty damn cluttered and noisy in my own head at times).

3. Realize that these types of thoughts once had a useful and valued purpose. If you were made to be wrong, or bad, or not good enough by some significant other in your childhood, the only way to really defend yourself was to beat yourself up before they could. (This is similar to jumping out of a car when you know it's going to crash. Yeah, it hurts, but at least it's not a head-on collision).

4. When these thoughts start to come up, immediately thank them for how they once protected you. Then remind them that you are just driving to work, and perhaps you don't really need to throw yourself out of the car door.

5. Do not argue with them, as they will only get louder and nastier.

6. Take ten minutes a day, and for two weeks, put these thoughts down on a piece of paper in writing. Note every conceivable defect, flaw, error and ugliness about your character, intelligence, appearance, aptitude and attitude.

7. At the end of ten minutes, take these thoughts that you have penned and destroy them. Rip them, flush them, burn them, and/or come up with your own unique disposal method.

8. If any other negative thoughts come up for you during the day, rest assured that you will have ample time to deal with them in an

appropriate way tomorrow. You can also thank them for sharing.

9. If this technique is ineffective for you, consult a trusted friend, therapist, religious advisor, or doctor. Find out what they do with their own crap and try it.

If despair is not just a vice, then hope is not just a virtue. At times it's allied with the belief in our own worthlessness...

Hope's Fault

We need to cherish the innocent.

Children, puppies, kittens, most all of the young and the young at heart are innocent. The innocent trust. They have no prejudice. The innocent hope. They have no expectations of doom, or loss, or shame or guilt. They are innocent. They are keeping the faith. When you are innocent with someone, you see him or her through the eyes of a child who trusts and hopes. If things turn out okay, you learn to value these qualities. If you are injured in this process you learn to pretend that trust and hope and faith are for fools.

I said, "learn to pretend," because most people find a way to keep the faith anyway. We learn the Golden Rule very early in life. From the church, or temple, or parents, or teachers. "If you are good, good things will happen. If you are bad, bad things will happen." – And, if you are good, and bad things happen, there is one absolute way to keep the faith.

Pretend you are bad. If you then act bad, and blame yourself, then it's all your fault. You caused it. Then there's a chance that you can "uncause" it, right? Hope and self-blame can be very close friends. The world will still make sense then. Then you can still hope, that maybe, just maybe, one day... – they will love you and support you.

It isn't so surprising that child molesters often die in prison. They are detested by the thieves, murderers and all other criminals. Perhaps the worst criminal act is murdering innocence. When innocence is corrupted, trust, hope and faith become tainted with our own self-denigration. We bury them in some deep crypt in ourselves. Some vault where they slowly suffocate. Some coffin where they scream and claw to be released.When we hear them, we add another nail to the coffin, another brick to the wall. We act in ways to harm others to justify why we ourselves were harmed. We protect the golden rule by becoming bad. Jail can be a safe place, you know. You see, when we stop blaming ourselves completely, and see those we want to love and care for us as incapable – we lose our self-blame.

Instead, we gain despair and depression. The truth is, it seems as if we have gone from purgatory (things could change if they're my entire fault) to hell (they will never change, no matter what I do). But we can get through this… Hope doesn't have to be blind.

If someone has harmed you, or others, I don't suggest that you blindly blame yourself, or them, or blindly forgive and forget. Innocence is important because it provides those we touch with it an opportunity, a chance for change. Innocence though, should not be confused with stupidity. As another innocent once said, "If a man strikes you on the cheek, do not strike back. Turn the other cheek to him." Well, we only have so many cheeks. As for me, three strikes, and you're out of here. For now. Hopefully, there may be other innings.

We need help in first learning to stand… and in learning to stand up for ourselves.

Standing On More or Less

Babies have to crawl or be carried. They don't have a choice. Their limbs are still too weak. The baby grows into the child without thinking much about it. There is magic here, as the "I" learns it has an impact on the world that is both self and others. We learn at first that we can move ourselves. So we do with great joy and enthusiasm.

When we finally get to stand on our own two feet, it is a wonder. You can imagine how proud the parents are – the encouragement they give. They are the strong, firm hands that help to guide our first few steps. These same hands help to cushion our fall. We all stumble at first, and teeter totter. When we are helping our child to learn to stand and walk, there are certain things we are careful about. We avoid teaching them in streets busy with traffic. We remove items that cause injury in the home. We sometimes provide a device allowing them mobility and balance while protecting them. We avoid pushing them down, tying them up, or imposing restraints that would impede their progress. Standing and walking make the child more independent.

As our body grows, so does the body of our intelligence, and the body of our emotions. We take in food for thought and food for the heart as well as nourishment for the physical self. We also need to learn how to balance and move these parts of us.

When we first stand up for what we feel, when we first stand up for what we believe in, are we given the same kind of support? Some of us are. Others are less fortunate. Some are taught to crawl instead of being taught to walk. Our feelings are ridiculed, or we are humiliated for attempting to think in any independent direction. For some of us, our ideas were never good enough, and the feelings we had were bad or wrong. So they thought for us, and felt for us. When we were with them, we found ourselves crawling. Consequently, any opportunity away from our parents was a chance to prove what we really did stand for, and how strong we really were.

As a matter of principle, away from them we refused to crawl at all. Choosing never to crawl showed everyone how grown up we really were. (Even if we never felt really grown up anyways). Away from them, we might become the parents to those we perceive as children. We might think for those, or feel for these whom we see as less than ourselves. We get to keep the illusion of being so much "more than" this way. The illusion is a blanket that protects and covers that little one inside us all.

We refuse to see and hear him or her inside. So we see the child outside, in everyone we meet, whether they are children or not. The help we offer can be healing for a time, but frequently cripples as much as it mends.

Parents make a baby. Parents make children, and children make parents. It's another deal. Adults get to make themselves. At times we need to choose to crawl, at times to stand and fight, at times to not even care if we care or not. Nobody can make you anymore. Yes, they can hurt you, or scare you, or rob you, rape you, or set you up to appear as if you were a fool. They can even kill you. They can please you, and flatter you, and attempt to seduce you. But they still don't make you who you really are.

No matter what it seems like they have reduced you to, or inflated you into, you are not that. You are what you choose to create out of each opportunity. No more, no less.

The hardest task in the world to accomplish is the strength of self-restraint.
  It's called ACCEPTANCE.

The Hard Part

I need to tell you about the hard part. The hard part is when someone's like a rose. You don't know what I mean yet. You just might in a little while, if you're patient. *Patient* means to persevere and endure calmly.
(No lie, it's from the dictionary). The hardest part is when someone's like a rose, when you really know

What Roses Are...
  Beneath the flower are those thorns. They protect and they can hurt you if you get too close. Her voice sometimes stings as sharp, and can wound. It's not her intent.
  Could you blame a rose for her thorns? Surely it is part of a nature that she had no choice about. Her body is stiff only to hold her head up high. It was kept down for so long as she waited for them. She was rooted, and only they could move. When she needed the warmth, the clouds were stormy. When she needed the shade, the light tried

to burn her. Who wouldn't grow thorns? It was almost always a desperate time. She had had it up to here. Right past her chin. All of her except the eyes. Her eyes were these buds that held promises never kept.

They glistened with a softness that still contained a trace of hope. Her lips had this kind of disdainful curl, pretending how much she didn't want to care. She pretended to pretend. But she cared too much. So here I am, real close to her now. And there appears to be nothing I can do. But if I do nothing, I will be like her former caretakers. They spent their time allowing her to wither. So I gently water her, and attempt to pull some of the weeds that choke her. And again, I remind her of *them*.

You see, when they woke up to what they starved her of, they flooded her with their guilt. These gestures nearly drowned her. Her thorns at least give points to all that was once so very pointless. There is only one thing to do. I look with her. At all the roots, and leavings, and at what stems from each branch of her being. Most especially I look with her eyes, and I let her see me doing it. When I look for too long, she feels her gut tighten into all the knots that tie her to the past, though I know she wants so much to be present. But she has Had It Up To Here with the world, and the past strangles the future she could see. We wait until she can catch her breath.

She catches enough to tell me of her hate for all the caretakers and gardeners of the world. She is sharp, this rose, so sharp that the thorns have stabbed her too. A price she paid in the scheme of things to survive. We look again together. She feels the venom and hate and unfairness of it all. She is this beautiful rose after all. Priceless.

And I hear the words she says to me, but I watch her eyes. They are the eyes of a child who has been betrayed. I want to touch her in some gentle way. She cringes when I draw near. So, I do the Hardest Part for me. The Most Loving Thing To Do For Now. I move away. Even though she is still starving, even though she is still in need. There is only so much she can take. There will be a Next Time soon. I will be patient. I know she will eventually blossom.

Because she is a rose.

*What appears to be crazy often makes all the sense in the world...
once you understand how to see it.*

Pushover

She got the bike for her tenth birthday. Like her, it was a beauty. Shiny chrome, metallic blue, ribbons from the handlebars. She could see herself flying with the wind. So could they. They could see her flying under a truck or over a car. They loved her and didn't want to lose her. They pretended that they never would, of course. So they told her with loud voices and in no uncertain terms,

"You are only allowed to ride in the driveway and in your own yard."

She begged and pleaded for the reason. Why? (She had learned at around five that Why worked much better than saying NO to them. "No" was cute at first, but they carried her off to bed and made her eat anyway. "Why" was usually good for at least 10 to 20 minutes of tactical delay).

Because, they said, you already know, that:

"You – don't obey."

"You – don't look or listen."

"You – don't think for yourself."

They thought they were making statements. But she heard them as commands. Loud voices always have the rank of generals.

So she obeyed them, as she wanted to be good. She obeyed them by not obeying, by not paying attention, and by not thinking for herself. And, naturally, the first thing she did the next morning was to attempt to ride the bike outside of her yard. Right at the very tiptoe end of the driveway she was. About to make the Great Escape. To be free, as free as the wind. When...

Bam. They knocked her off the bike.

They hurt her to prevent her from being hurt. "This is for your own good" battered what hadn't already been beaten. Perhaps this did save her, in some way. How was she to know? She just knew the pain and the desire to be free. She was a very determined and strong willed girl. So the next morning, she crept right to the edge, hopped on, and just about made it, when...

BAM! They knocked her down again. With more: "you don't listens," and "you don't obeys." So she didn't. And the next morning. BAM! And the next. BAM! And the next, and next and next and so on.

She knew they would knock her off. She was determined, though. She had to find a way to win. After the quadrillionth time, she got right to the tiptoe edge of the yard, hopped on the bike, and...immediately threw herself on to the ground. BAM! She beat them to it. At least she would fall the way she wanted. It was the only control she ever had, so she took it. She was no longer a pushover.

Later on in her life, just when she was about to achieve some form of success and independence, she always found some way to throw herself off. People wondered why she was so crazy, but it made perfect sense to me. Later on, when we saw what it was all about, she bought herself a brand new bike.

Man, that girl can ride...

Grieving is the process of healing a loss. There are effective ways to do this and a few are mentioned here.

Guidelines to Pain and Grief

1. There is necessary suffering all of us must go through in life. Pain cannot be avoided or resolved until it serves its purpose.

2. The function of pain is to identify that illness or injury is present and to motivate us to tend to our sickness and wounds. Although "feeling no pain" from intoxication may serve to reduce injuries in a traffic accident, it is likely they this condition helped create the harm in the first place.

3. Although anesthesia may be fine in the operating room for surgery, there is a natural condition that occurs where people who sustain gashes, cuts, and even broken bones don't ever have to feel their pain. This condition is the disease of leprosy. As a consequence, lepers are unaware of their wounds and injuries worsen, gangrene sets in, and irreparable damage to the body takes place.

4. Grief and sadness are the emotional equivalents to illness and injury. Grief occurs when there is an irreplaceable loss of persons or things that we have depended on for our well being. Grief should be allowed its course, and will manifest itself in feelings of sadness, anger, and depression.
Sadness, like other injuries, can originate through the slightest cut of negligence to the deepest wound of betrayal.

5. All of our injuries, no matter how small, require attention. In an emergency we may need to put our pain aside, for the sake of survival. Be advised that putting this care off for too long can create even more of a crisis later.

6. We can be in pain merely witnessing another's loss. However, if our hurt for the other is so great that it impedes our ability to help them, our pain in this instance is a manipulation. (If the victim or survivor of tragedy ends up comforting you, wake up, smell the coffee, and let someone more qualified be of assistance).

7. Crying alone is necessary at times. It does little good to share your grief with those who are non-receptive. It is equally important to allow others to share your sorrow. Pain is a heavy burden made lighter with other arms around you.

8. We may resist comfort at times simply because if we let someone else in we could lose them as well. This is similar to starving yourself to death in order to avoid being poisoned. (So take little sips of care if this is the case).

9. Crying produces natural endorphins that are pain relievers. A good cry is always helpful unless there are wild animals around who will take advantage of your vulnerability.

10. Our expressions of emotional pain are gender related. Most men learn to turn their hurt into anger. Most women are trained to turn their anger into pain. This prevents men from being comforted and women from asserting themselves. (This is a lousy deal for both sexes that can be changed if you simply reverse your typical response to frustration).

11. Pain and grief are very powerful tools used to heal, to convey need and, in turn, to get others to handle the ordinary responsibilities of the person who is hurt. Some are indeed helpless in being able to recover fully from certain types of illness and injury. Yet, some of us use pain as an excuse more than as a process of healing. For these folks, pain ceases to be a signal and becomes a permanent stop sign. The benefits of holding on to pain may need to be explored to open other roads of recovery and healing.

12. There are those of us too afraid to inflict or expose others to pain or grief. Here we can become surgeons who allow cancer to grow, judges who refuse to give sentences, coaches who let their teams get lazy and flabby, teachers who allow students to remain stupid, and friends who leave their other friends smiling with a big wad of spinach on their front teeth. Rethink your motives here.

13. Pain becomes unnecessary if right actions have been taken to tend to our wounds. This is why when we show up at the dentist's or doctor's the aches and pains sometimes disappear. They are simply no longer required. If all proper actions have been taken, and there is no relief, grief or depression may not be a psychological problem, but more of a biochemical imbalance.

"If man were meant to fly he would have been born with wings" is a bullshit statement made by people afraid to fly. We have discovered medicines and procedures that can do much to alleviate chronic pain and depression. Taking advantage of them makes you neither weak or drug dependent.

Using the resources you have to become well will empower both you and those you love.

The worth of any thought can be measured through the actions it promotes. Thoughts that negate create a vacuum that sucks our energy.

Adding Thoughts that Count

It's the thought that counts. I remember hearing that phrase whenever I received an unwanted gift; usually from someone defending someone else's neglect. We call the gift of not giving much thought at all – the thought that counts. Intent may not always produce the most beneficial results. Then again, I guess what that person "meant" to do really describes the absence of intent. A thought counts in this way only when I am doing a number on myself or somebody else. Numbers aren't "real," they are tools used to re-present some other aspect of reality. When thoughts negate or "not" the self, (not good, not smart, not caring, not creative, etc). we tie our motivation up into being less than who we are. This is rather useless for all concerned. If thoughts are going to be helpful they need to construct and to build upon. If we think we are "not good" the vacuum fills with thoughts of being "bad". If we are "not responsible," the vacuum fills with thoughts of being "irresponsible." If someone's "not black" does that mean they're Caucasian? If we are *not responsible* for the weather, does that make us irresponsible? The thoughts that count always add something that empowers. This includes the ones that describe our limitations as long as they are specific and accurate. The "NOTS" only tie us up. When you untie the "nots" you free the energy to become…all the thoughts that really count.

For most of us, the only conscious difference between garbage and recycled material is the container used for storage...

Remembering to Forget

I sometimes wonder how I can remember to forget about those little things that add up. You know, like leaving the toilet seat up, and my socks and underwear on the floor. (I think it would be better if we had our closets and drawers inserted directly in the bottom surface of any room. The force of gravity could help us put our stuff away). Evidently this is an idea practiced by all children carried around by their parents. After all, if you don't have to walk for yourself, you also don't have to trip over your own mess.

I also forget how to get where I'm going when I'm driving. I forget to wash that one glass in the sink. I get late and forget the time. Now, I could say that I'm just plain lazy, but I'm not. When I was single, I really don't remember pulling these same tricks. Maybe when you are dating you put that best foot forward. After you are really sure he or she is The One, then you can begin to remember how to forget for both of you. You know, if I had to diagnose myself, I would have to say that these behaviors of mine were passive aggressive. This is a shrink term for helplessness that has the unconscious intent of getting someone else to be pissed off at you. Supposedly, whoever enacts this as a pattern also has difficulty expressing their anger.

So, we set the other up to come down on us, and give us these verbal reprimands. It may make it that much easier to get pissed-off back.

All of this may contain an element of truth. It's much easier to get angry with someone if they are beating on you. So we can play pass the aggression, fire the torpedo, full speed ahead. Sounds right. Pieces fit nicely. Simple. Logical, etc., etc.. Here we assume that an adult has the power to make another adult act in a certain way. It's that whole cause-effect trip again. The *I-make-you* so that *you-can-*

make-me theory. All of it is about *the Me, myself and I*. I don't think so. I think it's all about *Us*. About relationships.

Here's an idea. For every passive-aggressive there's an aggressive-passive. This would be a person afraid to express their vulnerability in some area. So, they always have to remember. They are not allowed to forget. They always have to be on time, pick up every piece of lint, and not only do the last dish, but also remember to cometize the sink. They find someone who is passive aggressive like me who can be real pathetic in these matters. It's much easier to get helpless with someone who, no matter how many times you remind them, simply forgets.

Eventually the aggression deflates to this futility of accepting life with the brain damaged. After you have exhausted all threats, you cry to them for understanding and release. You see, all of these little things add up to getting my wife to Correct me.

In "correct," you may read nag, scold, bitch, and take on an air of authority. She gets her opportunity to show me how I'm not as perfect as all of those people (including me) think I am. And I, well, I get to be a little kid at that moment. Taken care of. I get attention, and structure, and security, and yes, even love. If, of course, she steps over the line in this process, as in verbal abuse, I get an additional "win" at my own expense. I get to change the subject and be a righteous bastard attacking her for being a righteous bitch. Don't you just hate those people who think that they are so much better than you? (All the while knowing that you are way better than them for not doing what they do). She, of course, gets to finally be helpless in even attempting to get me to be responsible.

The difficulty in this game is that neither one of us gets any respect or positive reaction for being powerful or vulnerable. It's just stuff we throw at each other, instead of being with each other. Now I know that this may all be a major rationalization. The truth is I could just be a slob. Or, my wife and I have different definitions of the concept "mess." Another truth is, everyone needs a time and place where they can feel in control.

Everyone may need a time and place where they can trust another to make it secure for them. Where you don't have to think for yourself. We all get a chance to pick the songs that we want to dance to. The most likely truth of all is that there is a harmony hidden in the tune. Even if we aren't quite playing in the same key.

QUESTIONS ON TRUST

1) When is hope a virtue and when is it a vice?

2) What is consistently inconsistent in your life?

3) How much time do you waste trying to change stuff not really under your control? – What do you avoid changing instead? (I didn't say we should give up "influencing." Differentiate the two. It might include lowering unrealistic expectations in order to take realistic actions).

4) If you won't abandon anyone at anytime – who the hell abandoned you?

5) If you take offense at that last question, why would you not abandon those who still felt entitled to hurt you, and you couldn't really stop them?

6) Does love always have to include everyone?

7) If you answered yes, are you included in the love you give, or are you just trying to be loved by being loving?

HEY YOU!

Yeah, YOU!

Wanna be STRONG?

Wanna be POWERFUL?

Of course you do.

The greatest strength we have as humans abides in the power of our flexibility.

(Which of course, – includes being an authority, a subordinate and both once).

Here's how to do them all...

（装飾罫線）

Chapter 3: Gaining Power and Control

Most of us want to be strong. We want to be right. We want to be in control. We want to be better than we were, or better than somebody else. We want to be able to predict what will happen when we take some action.

We don't realize that most of our notions about being powerful come from the fantasies and experiences of our childhood. Here we first learned how to hold on and how to let go. Much of what we learned is repeated whenever we attempt to structure our lives and manage our time getting things in order. In fact, the whole notion about what "order" is comes from these echo's of our past. Some of us hang on to the idea that we aren't really together unless we do everything perfectly. Some of us live in a constant mess, and can't seem to put things in place if our lives depended on it.

Our anger and aggression can be very confusing to us here. Some revel in being able to express it, and some avoid it like the plague. Some of us are terrified of losing control; others are terrified of gaining it. We either get afraid of being called judgmental, or we get afraid of being considered a rug that anyone can walk on. The end result of all of these experiences is usually shame, doubt, and humiliation.

The guides and stories in this chapter are about these conflicts. Here you will learn to differentiate the behaviors of power and control. (Yes, they are two different things). You'll learn when to drive yourself and when to allow someone else to take the wheel. There are concepts and tools to assist you in dealing with shame and humiliation in your life. You'll also learn where and when force is useful, as well as useless.

Our patterns of holding on and letting go will be explored in depth. What truly makes us powerful has little to do with how much money or possessions or status we accumulate, and everything to do with how we use what we do have.

The riches we really need to earn are the process and tools that allow us to achieve our goals in the first place. Like a sturdy tree, our strength needs to come from maintaining a stable structure flexible enough to bend with the winds of change. Hopefully, this chapter will enable you to empower both yourself and others in this manner.

Power is not so much the end goal as it is the means for achieving it...

Acceptance and Making

We can see two basic forces at work in an automobile. The force of *power* comes from the engine. The force of *control* comes through the steering wheel, gears and brakes. Without them, we cannot drive. We can have the best controls in the world. We can have the most sophisticated brakes, steering and pedals ever designed. Without the power of the engine they are useless devices that serve no function. It doesn't matter how powerful the engine is if we can't stop or direct our movement.

So, we must use both forces together if we are to safely reach a destination. There are the same two forces we use to deal with the world. Power is about internal *acceptance*. Our power as humans comes from the *acceptance* of our emotions and imagination. We must be able to feel *what is* and imagine *what could be*. Acceptance is the action of *internal* real-ization. For the moment we let go of our musts, have-tos and shoulds-to perceive both the path that is, and the paths that just might be. Acceptance only becomes possible when we detach from external goals and become receptive to our feelings and imagination.

Making is about *control*. Making is the push/pull, the holding on and letting go, the use of all our muscles and effort. Making is the action of external real-ization. Making is the step that creates a path that was first only seen in our mind. Through our making, the path becomes a road, the road a highway. Through our making, the sitting becomes crawling becomes walking becomes running becomes riding becomes flying. Making comes from the directed use of our intellect and physical self.

It is our passion and needs that motivate us and energize our movement.

Our imagination fuels the possibilities of fulfillment. To gain this power we must allow ourselves to feel and dream...

To gain control, we must put our passions and needs aside to focus on the task at hand. Here we should and must make ourselves think and sense...

Most of us are pretty good at one or the other. To get good at both we need to learn how to shift. This is where neutral comes in...

To have a goal of not having a goal is impossible, or so it seems with words. How can one be in neutral? – By releasing the clutch...

Driving with Neutral

Okay – most of you are familiar with a stick shift in a car. The stick shift operates in conjunction with a clutch. You step on the clutch to disengage from one gear to engage with another gear. We shift when we need to slow down or speed up. Perhaps there is a hill, and we need to switch to a lower gear to have enough power to make it over the top. Perhaps we need to accelerate in a higher gear to avoid an accident.

We do something quite similar within ourselves. At times, we may have to deliberately shift between emotional states. Anger may not be an appropriate response and we're more likely to get our needs met by becoming vulnerable. Or, vulnerability gets us nowhere and we need to put or foot down. Or, we're being too passionate and need to think instead.

So we need to shift our internal gears. When we detach from a gear we are in neutral. When we attach to a gear we are in first, second, third, fourth, or reverse. To detach, we simply step on the clutch. We release what we have been holding onto. That gear was perfectly all right to drive in...until *Now*. In this *Now* we may need a different form of power and control to get us where we want to go.

In Eastern philosophy a great deal of emphasis is placed on detachment as a spiritual process. When we detach from desire, we are relieved from unnecessary suffering. However, we must also be able to detach from our indifference. Those with the burning *desire to be detached from desire* mostly ride around in neutral. Neutral is good for shifting between gears and may be effective when you have run out of gas to coast downhill. It can also be good when your battery is dead so that you can pop the clutch. For the most part, we need to use neutral as a tool to disengage only to re-engage in a different way.

Acceptance allows movement. The engine runs the car. (Our feelings and imagination motivate us). Making moves acceptance. The control gives us a direction. (Our thoughts and senses direct our feelings and imagination). Detachment allows us to direct the process of control.

When we make ourselves physically or mentally enact a behavior, we need to let go of the outcome, and focus on what is in our control. Our goal may be to effect something in the environment. We must *first* effect ourselves to accomplish this task. This is practice, getting the strokes right. You swimmers and golfers and ballplayers know what I mean. When we have managed to do these movements without any intent to do them "right," then we can allow ourselves to detach from technique, and use all of the other strengths we have.

If we ride our clutch, it will burn out. If we don't use neutral at all, the gears will grind into uselessness. In both cases, we will lose control of the controls that we have at our disposal. Sometimes you have to gear up. Sometimes you have to gear down. As you will soon see...

Learning to shift is an important aspect of any drive...

Gears and Roles

As a therapist, I'm often asked what I think my role is. I usually reply "Danish sourdough." When people ask me for my astrological sign, I often respond with "Slippery When Wet." I suppose I do this because I am at times, a smart-ass, and because I don't want to get pinned down and labeled. If it's one thing that I've learned as a psychotherapist, it is that people are never any one "thing."

Roles are often like the gears to the car. In my life, I have three basic "gears" or roles that you can see. I have first gear, which is a gear of vulnerability. I have second gear, which is a gear of authority. And finally, I have third gear, which is a gear of equality.

The interesting thing I have discovered is that each role has within it a multitude of similar characters. My gear of vulnerability is something I need to shift into when someone else is responsible for me. Here I allow myself to be like a "child." As a child, I make myself listen, follow directions, ask for support and direction, and generally receive from the other. Related roles in this gear are the student, the employee, the patient, the client, the congregation member, and virtually any position that requires playing a subordinate. For me to be in first gear, I need somebody else to be in second gear, the gear of authority. When I am in a role of authority, I am doing so because I am responsible for the actions of others. I may be acting like a "parent."

I may also play teacher, boss, minister, doctor, judge, coach, or any other gear that is similar to these. When I am in this process I make myself direct, decide, and demand. I make myself take charge in some way. In order to do so, I must have someone who is in the dependent gear.

You see, on this road we're on, well, we are never alone. We may not always be able to see ahead, or behind, but you can bet that someone's on that road with you. When we shift gears, it's not just because of the nature of the hills and valleys along the way. A lot of shifting is because of the other traffic. It doesn't matter at the moment that you may have the right of way.

It matters how the other person is driving. In order to be vulnerable, we must be with another who is in authority. In order to be an authority, we must be with another who is vulnerable. If we are with those in authority that do not meet our needs, we may need to shift from a child to a student, or to other aspects of that first gear. There is a responsibility in vulnerability. We must follow. There is a concurrent responsibility in being an authority. An authority must direct, and direct in a manner that fosters compliance without damaging capability. We cannot be an authority with someone who isn't receptive to following us.

If they are not, perhaps we need to allow ourselves to shift into third gear, a process of equality. This may at first seem like neutral, as there is no making or force relative to another. This is the role that allows others to make themselves. There is still a goal, however. The goal is that we make ourselves instead of attempting to make the other. We can act *with* another in this role.

The gear of equality is best seen in the role of an adult. Parents and children are "for" each other. Adults are for themselves and "with" each other. Other gears within this frame may be friend, husband, wife, peer, associate, or colleague. A friend is not responsible for his friend, but is responsible for maintaining behaviors that are "friendly." A husband is not responsible for his wife, but is responsible for behaviors that can help maintain his marriage. In this gear of equality, we only have to answer to and for what we have mutually agreed upon. It is not a matter of right and wrong (as is the case in vulnerability and authority). Here it is truth and consequences.

If I see you as a peer, than you are just as capable as I am in deciding or doing for yourself. You still have the choice to ask or demand, and then we may shift gears again.

We cannot hold onto our happiness. But we can shift and allow ourselves to enjoy it, – even if you think you are a loser…I have something for you folks to ponder next.

This particular piece is for all of us who always seem to screw up.

Perfect Mistakes

There are some positions we take that we really need to reconsider:
   I will always fail.
   I am always wrong.

If you are caught up in thinking that you will always be unsuccessful in everything you attempt, there is some hope for you. Sooner or later you will fail in being unsuccessful. I'm sorry, but it's true. I know that this may ruin an otherwise perfect and consistent record on your part. But if failing is all you ever do, it can't be helped.

You will fail at failing, too. (You people who always succeed will, of course, have those victories of defeat to teach you humility and empathy).

And for those of us filled with doubt and shame, there is a way out. If you are always wrong, well, eventually you will be wrong about being wrong. Eventually, you can have so much doubt that you begin to doubt how much doubt you really have. Then you can begin to realize that all of your mistakes have been made quite correctly. As a matter of record, you made perfect mistakes. When you were wrong, you made them right. When you were stupid, you made them smart. When you were sick, they had to be healthy. Perhaps they needed the distraction, so you gave them the opportunity to yell, or play hero, or whatever. (How nice of you to be so thoughtful). Remember that you could take care of them in another way that will still be good for both of you.

However, if you really feel the need to be perfectly consistent in failing, you can use this little verbal game with people. Simply say "Whatever I do with you, I'm going to be wrong." If they say "You're right," you get to be wrong. If they say "You're wrong," point out, that, one more time, they are making you wrong. However, knowing you, you'll find some way to screw this up.

Perfectly. Some of you are out there saying, "Yeah, – but," The next story has your name on it.

Here's a story about one of my clients who also desired physical perfection. Little did she know how her concern with her flaws was all part of the plan...

Large Butts

Some of us are concerned about the shape and size of our bodies. We compare ourselves to others, look in the mirror, and obsess about specific portions of our anatomy. There may be some truth to our concerns. There may also be a truth different from what we see...What we perceive as being too small or too big is also a message. (From the back of our minds to the front).

I had a beautiful young woman who came to see me for therapy. She was upset about the size of her posterior, – her behind, her buttocks, her rump. She thought her ass was way too big. Every morning she would wake up, look in the mirror, and chastise herself for her big butt. She would fret about it, worry about it, diet and exercise like crazy.

She couldn't perceive anything changing, so she came in to see me. I asked her to stand and turn around. Her butt was smaller than average for her height and weight, and nicely shaped. I told her so, and she responded with, "But it's not." I knew it was useless to argue at this point, so I began to offer suggestions that would be helpful in the way she wanted help. I offered alternative exercises. "But," she responded, "I already tried those." I offered alternative diets. "But," she responded, "I can't do that." I offered every alternative that I could imagine. Each suggestion was negated with a "But...." She was right. She had a very big But and a tendency to make an ass out of herself.

When it dawned on me just exactly where this big but really existed for her, I shared the observation. We both saw her big But then. In her requesting help, and consequently rejecting any direction derived from that request, she was able to be in control. From that moment on, she worked on reducing the size and extent of her but. She still has a nice one. Not too big, and not too small. So, if you are concerned with the size of your posterior, bear this in mind.

If you perceive your penis or breasts as too small, maybe you need to look where and when you're acting like a kid. If you perceive yourself as overweight, perhaps you are carrying more responsibility for others than you should. The difference between what is your mind and what is your body is in your mind.

Your "brain" is not just in your head, it exists wherever you have neurons, or nerve cells. All neurons, including those in your head and body are identical in structure. This means your mind is in every part of you. Even your butt. So listen to what you might be trying to say. Every picture tells a story, even if it's pure garbage.

Refusing to push ourselves that little extra bit can create a stink...

Taking Out the Garbage

Thursday night is garbage night. My chore.

After working hard all day, I usually pull up in the driveway, grateful to be home and *finally* relax. The garbage cans are two feet away. It would take me all of two minutes to complete the job.

But, come on, I deserve a break. I'm tired. I've worked pretty damn hard this week. Besides, I'll get up in the morning and do it. Naturally, I just miss the morning round. I hear the truck coming and I move like a bat out of hell. My heart is moving faster than my feet in that adrenaline rush. I watch the truck pull away.

Shit. Now I have two weeks of garbage.

Thursday night is garbage night. My chore.

After working hard all day, I pull up in the driveway again. I see two weeks of garbage.

More work. But, come on, I deserve a break. I'll get them in the morning. I'll wake up extra early, and catch that truck if it kills me. Really. I'll set the alarm an hour early.

Only seconds have passed as I wake up to this awful buzzing. I look at the time. Shit. Some idiot set the alarm an hour early. I appreciate that full extra hour of rest. Ha. Ha. I close my eyes.

Thursday night is garbage night. There are three weeks of garbage in my driveway. I'm tired. I can't pull the car into the driveway. There's too much garbage. I park in the street. I'm going to get that garbage out tonight, *Right After Dinner!* I swear. During dinner, I hear the sound of a car crashing on my street. Right in front of my house. I run out, and...

Yep. My damn car. Some idiot hit my car. Hit and run. I get the license anyway. I'm up late with the police and insurance, and arranging rides. Of course, I forget…

Thursday night is garbage night. My chore. There is six months of garbage in my driveway, on my front lawn, in my bedroom, in my kitchen, in my bathroom. Everywhere. I don't entertain much these days.

As a matter of fact, I finally decided to move out of this piece of crap home I live in. You can just never keep it clean. I'm moving to a nice clean house just a few blocks away. Today.

Monday night is garbage night on my new block. My chore.

You know, Monday is just about the hardest day of the week to work. When I get home on Monday, I usually just pull up in the driveway, grateful to be home, and happy to relax for a while. Come on, I deserve it. I work hard all day long. I'll just get up early the next day. Really.

Nobody has power over you unless you allow it. Here are some reasons why we blame ourselves for others' behavior…

The Cause

Looks aren't everything, you know.

Unless you are one of those types who can "make" everyone turn their head to look at you when you pass by. If you are, then I'm sure you have those days when you are *soooooo* ugly that when you pass by, you "make" everybody look away. When people look in your direction, how the hell can you be sure that it's really about you?

Sometimes you are just a target for some trigger-happy marksman who is disposing surplus ammunition. Bullets of love and hate that fell the innocent bystander. Arrows from Cupids with difficulties of glandular excess. Hooks from greedy fishermen out angling. Going for those suckers. Missionaries saving the lost souls for God. (I assume when you save enough souls, you can turn them in like coupons for the Grand Prize of Heaven).

We are all in season for hunters who are starving. Most don't require a license to be hungry. Just an emptiness is necessary. It is very easy to become a Thing for another to use. All you have to do is forget who you are. All you have to do is pretend that you will be paid back. All that you have to do is to give up your faith in something more than yourself. All that you have to do is buy into the belief that you are the Cause. Yes, the Cause.

Being the Cause for an other's behavior means assuming that:
    1) You are making them do what they do.
    2) Since you are making them, you are in control of their behavior.
    3) You should also be able to stop them from doing what they are doing, as you are responsible for their actions in the first place.

It seems to be a very powerful position.

"Seems" is the operative word here. Even our weakness can appear to be powerful. Being a target does get us a kind of attention, doesn't it? But who said that you drew the arrow to you? The archer had some choice in the matter. There are some waters that are shark infested, with no signs posted. You can be in the water for a long time, and if the sharks have fed, you are safe. Don't think that this has anything to do with you. If they are still hungry, you are shark bait. However, this doesn't mean that we are totally off the hook in this Cause business.

We all use Causes to justify our actions. Here we are attempting to make behavior reason-able. "It happened because…" (Here we can substitute a reason that fits with the an other's beliefs, so that they will accept us and what we did). You do Cause something that relates to the other's behavior. We all do. We all "cause" *Opportunity*, just by being in a particular where and when. An opportunity is a potential.

You get an illusion of power as you connect with all those people who give you whatever type of looks sounds, or actions that are, of course, *Because of You*…Because then, we can Control the behavior that "made" them act like they did. We can make ourselves do more of it to get the good stuff. We can make ourselves do less of it, and avoid the bad stuff.

Okay, now let me play devil's advocate here. Suppose you don't "cause" anybody to do anything. So you go up to a stranger and insult them. Doesn't that "cause" them to become aggressive? If you strike a child, doesn't that cause them to feel abused? Perhaps. You could be hired to insult someone at a Hollywood "Roast."

The child you strike could be sticking a fork into an electrical outlet, and your "hitting" them may break the flow of electricity. Surgeons stick knives into people everyday. (Only a few have to be criminally prosecuted. Many are thanked for slicing people). You see, all our "reasons" for doing things help create what we call a "context." A context is the sequence of actions that surround a specific event. When you make rules for cause and effect outside of these contexts, you get to believe that your rules will keep you safe, or make your situation better. Well, they could, or they might. Then again, they just might not.

We do create the *OPPORTUNITY* for other people's behavior. Laws create the opportunity for justice. They can be used for injustice as well. If you believe you can manipulate people to sing the kind of songs that they sing, well, you might be right. You can create the opportunity. But, you don't make them, anymore than you made the record, or disc, or videocassette. You just learned how to play them. Now, you just may be an artist who did compose the music, or paint the picture, or create the film. We do "cause" some of our *own* songs and pictures. You do "make" some of your own behavior. Some of it.

Most of the body of our work is an adaptation from the novel experiences we go through as children, from other recordings, other pictures, other films. We do "make" children. We do "cause" children. They record most everything, to be replayed when they find the right player. These tunes can drive them to drink, or love, or to be cruel and sadistic. These tunes can drive all of us.

Causality with people is a lot different than causality with Things. (Even when you perceive other people as Things to use as Opportunities). We all have these recordings of guilt, and fear, and shame. We also have recordings of initiative, and confidence, and pride. As adults we get to change the stations that we have listened to. What we really cause for other grown-ups is opportunity. What we really create for children is their Cause.

Exercises in futility are excellent vehicles for avoiding the important...

Watering the Astro-turf

God is supposedly All Knowing. Must have already heard every joke ever spoken – And every one that ever will be told. Already seen play and movie ever done. Must be boring. Maybe that's a good reason for how we humans came to be. Free will and all that. We humans can at least choose the unexpected.

Just when you thought you had it all under control, you get...a pie in the face. Laughter is the great equalizer. It transforms the pathetic and the powerful into all of us Bozos On the Bus. Everything that we are terrified of, everything that we are shamed by, we can also learn to laugh at. We can even laugh at death. Humor is that magic that transforms the lead of existence into golden moments that lift and lighten our hearts.

Most men spend nine months in a woman's womb, take a break for sixteen or so years, and then spend the rest of their lives trying to put at least part of their anatomy back inside. (Or in searching for larger breasts). The more obsessed they are in these activities, the more "manly" they are. (As opposed to being bigger babies, of course).

Parents believe that they can "instruct" their children to behave independently. I mean, if they do everything you tell them, are they independent? Every parent who I know who does have "independent" kids that wants to see if the hospital screwed up with the birth certificate. It's like that with commercials on television. Real grown-ups use Ban roll-on, drive Fords, drink Coors, and eat Swanson's

Hungry Man frozen dinners. (Only those who can truly think for themselves).

Fighting for peace? Come on. It's like having the death penalty to "preserve the sanctity of human life." We fight for Piece. A piece of this, a portion of that. Some parents had the rule "One of you can divide this in half, and the other gets first choice." I wonder if we could fancy this up in proper official language and use it instead of bullets. How about those people who water the astro-turf? There they are, every morning. When you mention the futility of ever getting that plastic to grow, you get this blank stare. The look that you're given implies that you're the one who has missed something here, bub. After all, it certainly stays green, doesn't it? What all of this comes down to for me is that there is no such thing as futility.

Futility has a purpose. Futile actions have this purpose of helping us avoid *What We Are Most Afraid To Attempt.* Besides watering the astro-turf, we enter all sorts of dead end relationships with people and things.
These are some of my special favorites:

1) *Searching for the Holy Grail of Motivation.*

Here we can avoid something we need to do by first searching for a good reason to do it. This can take years if you really apply yourself. An excellent choice. Fruity, yet with a sour aftertaste of blown opportunities.

Another item on the menu, a personal favorite of mine, is a combination of selections:

2) *Painting Appreciation for the Blind and/or Music Recitals for the Deaf.*

Attempting to display your capabilities in these areas can waste ample time. The essential and necessary mind-set required for an ongoing commitment is self doubt and denial. You can then proceed to avoid by presenting a sequence of larger and larger works. The first canvass may have been too small, or too lightly drawn. Try a larger picture, a louder symphony. When you finally bring that hundred foot billboard in harsh neon accompanied with the five hundred marching band members...and they Still Don't Get It...well...Then you still get to be not good enough without actually risking being truly heard or seen. This dish is recommended for those with a hearty appetite for martyrdom followed by a chaser of persecution for the people they tried to save.

The expression that covers this is, "Get off the cross, Jesus. We Need The Wood!"

3) *Being Afraid to be Afraid.*

(Well, it's never too late to really worry about something that has already happened, that you can do nothing about). Like I said, you can get a lot of mileage here away from where you could be going. The only thing to fear is fear itself has a nice ring to it if you like circles. Rings are circles that go around and around. Me, I'm not afraid of being afraid. I appreciate fear. Fear helps me to run away from out-of-control vehicles and mad dogs.

4) *Trout fishing in the Sahara Desert, or actually, farming in the Sahara Desert, or Tanning in Antarctica in a snowstorm, or spitting into the wind in front of you.*

I don't believe that these need any real explaining. (If you duck quickly enough after you spit, you can most likely hit the first person coming up behind you).

5) *Wondering if God can do anything, since God is God after all, can God also create a rock so big that not even God could move it?*

Personally, I think that you should let God answer that one in God's own way. Which leads me back to cosmic jokes and astro-turf. Any time I begin to question the futility of existence these days, I'll have to wonder if God was really avoiding doing something else when God created the Universe. If life is really futile, then it's up to you me to make a purpose then, isn't it? Perhaps it's all really in The

Plan after all. Those who water the astro-turf develop remarkable accuracy with the hose. Perhaps they become excellent firefighters. Or something else. Maybe in our journeys of avoidance we pick up on some skills we never would have otherwise. But, once you got them down, maybe it's time to get the hell out of there.

You can't walk away from any "here" unless you are concurrently walking towards a different "there". Part of the process may include falling...

A Simple Way to Move

Did you know that a baby learns to walk as a by-product of falling? Walking is, at first, a series of forward falls. Going on requires this step. Any step is three related actions:

First, we lift a foot.

Second, we let go of our weight and fall forwards. (Gravity helps here).

The third aspect is putting that foot that was extended down on the ground again.

As we do so we plant our weight and balance to the new ground we have gained. If we plan to continue our progress we do the same procedure with the other foot. To move: extend, let go-hold on...extend, let go-hold on...Jumping up and down will not change your position. It will just create a depression that you'll have to climb out of anyway. Could be an excellent dance that also keeps you in the same place.

Fine – if you like where you're at. To move: extend, let go-hold on...extend, let go-hold on...Etceteras. Got it? Good. Now let go of it. You'll hold on to it with another part of you.

You can now assert yourself towards another direction.

Our teeth and nails are a part of our genetic inheritance. We need them. Our aggression is not an evil force, just another tool. At the very least we can learn to fight with skill and integrity...

Guidelines to Aggression and Assertion

1. Anger is an emotion that motivates us to control others, situations, or events when we are frustrated in fulfilling our needs or achieving goals. Our anger does not need to be justified, but the means we use to express our aggression does. (The end never justifies the means). Assertion is one means of channeling anger in a manner that avoids abusing or diminishing the other.

2. Unrestricted aggression is called rage. We first have to find our temper; how stupid of us to lose it again when found. Assertion is handling the tool of aggression in a directed and restrained way. This is called strength. Never use a sledgehammer when a fly swatter will do. Otherwise you make costly holes that breach your security.

3. Anger is neither immoral nor indicative of poor mental health. It is an essential emotion that can motivate us to govern our own lives. It is rather useless in if it is directed towards events we have no control over in the first place. Yet, once our anger emerges it must be directed outwards in a productive manner. This is why sports in general are so popular. Here we can beat, kill, and smash the other players with our clubs and bats. (And we can have a ball in doing this in more ways than one).

4. Those of us who blindly condemn aggression were most likely victims of it in our childhood. We become afraid to be like the aggressor that hurt us. One danger here is swallowing our anger until we begin projectile vomiting. Then, as the dam collapses, we rage and become what we were most afraid of being. The solution here is to let your feelings be known the moment you are aware of whatever injustice or frustration you experience. This may not change the situation, but

it will always change you.

5. Pacifists and fascists support each other in that fascists *live* by the motto "Might makes right," and pacifists *die* by that same motto. As much as I prefer the nonviolent perspective as an ideal, in conflicts with the violent most pacifists are left to act peacefully dead. There is a major difference between the aggression of a mass murderer who destroys lives and the policeman who fights to save lives.

6. The difference between "I'm pissed at you because..." and "You stupid asshole" is the difference between assertion and aggression. If the person you are abusively labeling has any regard for your opinion, they will follow your direction. If those around you act as *dumb, incompetent, inadequate, clumsy, good for nothing, foolish, lazy, lying, sneaky, slovenly, unimaginative, thieving, wimpy, ungrateful pieces of shit*, consider that they just may be following your orders. Consider what your investment is in helping to keep them that way.

7. Raising your voice in an assertive manner is no more abusive than having the color red appear at a stoplight. I would suggest that you use the yellow "proceed with caution" signal prior to this when at all possible. (There are those of us who always sneak through the yellow, and run the red anyway, so further action may be required. By the way, you can't "make" them stop anyway).

8. Assertive actions call for you to take care of your needs without exploiting or being unjust to others. If there is abusive or neglectful behavior taking place that angers you, the following steps may be applicable:
a) Express to the other in specific terms what is abusive or neglectful about their behavior.
b) Express how it makes you feel and what it makes you think.
c) Give them some consequences for this behavior if it occurs in the future. These can range anywhere from a reprimand to legal action.

d) Carry out those consequences.

9. The strongest and most assertive action you can take in any relationship is to leave. Use this as a last resort if all else fails. Your well being and self respect are not to be sold out for security, power, freedom, money, fame, or love. The only thing in life that can't be taken from us is our integrity. If you sell it, you sell your soul. (And believe me, it's a bitch to buy back).

If too much security becomes a jail, and too much freedom renders us homeless, the proper balance between the two hinges on...

Walls and Openings

A wall can protect us. Unless, of course, our back is up against it, and what is threatening us has us cornered. Then the security of the walls and the room become a trap. Then what could save us would be an opening. An opening can protect us. Unless, of course, what is threatening us is faster and stronger. Then we wish we had that damn wall we tore down to escape. If we just live in the open we are free to catch our death of cold. We can be trapped in our security and we can be just as trapped in our freedom. It's the all or nothing routine that gets us there.

Me? Well, I don't choose to use either. Actually I use a combination of both. When you add a wall and an opening together you get a Door. A Door is a moveable wall. A Door is a close-able opening. A door hinges on both the inside and the outside. A door needs to be solid in its substance and fluid in it's movement. When it is open, it is a gateway. When shut, it is a wall. My door hinges on what the whether is inside and outside. *Whether* I can let the outside in or the inside out in a way that's mutually rewarding. If I can, my door's open. If I can't – it's closed.

I guess I'm an open and shut case.

Arrogance always involves a comparison with someone else. Pride is more self contained...

Feeling Something Better

I caught myself in the mirror tonight. You know. When you look at your reflection and see something that puts you above everyone else. When you see something special, and you say to yourself, Ahh. *If They Only Knew What I Know.* The world could be a much, much better place.

So, going with this feeling, I wondered what it was that I knew so much better than anyone else. Then it hit me, right at that moment of self-reflection. What I knew so much better than anyone else was...*That I am one hell of an arrogant person to think that I knew better than everyone else.* By this time I figured that everyone else who knows me also knows this anyway, too. To save face I turned off the bathroom light and went to bed. To hug my wife. Really, to have her hug me.

I only look to see how big I am when I am afraid that I may be too small. (And usually end up deflated when the balloon of my ego pops). She hugged me. I didn't feel better. I felt good. You have to feel worse in order to feel better. I've come to the conclusion that feeling good is even better than feeling better. There's just no comparison.

QUESTIONS ON POWER AND CONTROL

1. What are the differences between power and control?

2. What feelings push you? What dreams pull at you?

3. How do you focus your energy when you've taken on a task?

4. Where and when would it make you strong to admit you were weak?

5. Where and when would it be weak (let alone stupid) to try to prove your strength?

6. Where and when and with who do you need to act with authority right now in your life?

7. Where and when and with who do you need express your vulnerability right now in your life?

8. Who have you been treating as an authority or a child that you really need to treat as an adult?

9. How do you stop yourself from changing this?

10. What could you now do instead?

WHO are YOU?
***WHO* do you think *YOU* are?**

**A rose by any other name won't always smell as
sweet if the name really stinks...Identity. Identify.
We are not MORE than what we think.
We are *DIFFERENT* from what we think.**

**We can use those differences to grow.
Here's how.**

Chapter 4: The Secrets of Identity

It's interesting to note that most heroes from the comics have a "secret identity". In their heroic role, men and women have powers far beyond those of us mere mortals. In their "normal" identities, many of these folks are meek and mild klutzes who can't tie their own shoelaces without help.

You know, we don't really *find our Self* as much as we *make and allow our Self.* Many don't know this because they've spent a lifetime trying to *make other people...* – love them, like them, respect and accept them. (Most were unsuccessful. If they did manage to achieve this illusion, they were quite unsatisfied). "Making" someone else act a certain way towards us implies that his or her regard was forced. Choice is of the essence here. Without choice, the value of friendship and love is diminished. When we learn to accept both our vulnerabilities and strengths, so we enter into the realm of being able to make choices. Children have no choice but to be helpless at times, and concurrently, parents may have no choice but to be strong. Adults can choose both positions and then some.

We may need to set boundaries that shelter us from urges that can be destructive to others. At the same time, we have to manifest passion and drive to satisfy our own needs. How we reconcile this conflict has a lot to do with the heroes we identify with, and the villains we despise. Values and ethics become important here, as they serve to maintain a consistent way of being.

In order to choose, we must acknowledge these needs and the resources available to fulfill them. We have to embrace our own and others capabilities and limitations to accomplish this task.

To "identify" anything is to name it. Names have power.

To "identify with" somebody or something is to merge with this "other" and call it our own. This is pretty easy to do with what we identify as "*good.*" But there are so many behaviors that we cannot imagine ourselves being or doing. Some call this aspect of the Self "*SHADOW.*" These are unwanted thoughts, feelings and sensations that we are afraid to experience within ourselves. They have little to do with being good or evil. Here false guilt and anxiety bind us to convictions that are little more than jail sentences locking up choice. On the other extreme, those with no guilt at all may justify doing anything to anyone for their personal gain.

This chapter is about balance. Here you will learn about going from one extreme to the other in order to find the middle ground. There are guides that deal with values and virtues, and how to form them. You' ll also learn that colors *and* black and white are all necessary, and a part of the larger picture. Your problems can be solutions to other difficulties. We discuss sexuality and what it means to be an adult. There are tips for learning how to sail smoothly in life, without having to cut loose your responsibilities. We can discover the difference between true and false guilt, and learn to use both.

In short, we're dealing with the secrets of identity – how we make and allow ourselves to become adults.

If our SELF has a coherent structure, our values are the vessel that maintain it.

Guidelines to Values

1. What is valuable in one situation may be completely worthless in another. A million dollars in cash is worth less than a glass of water if you are dying of thirst in the desert.

2. There is potential worth in every object and process if we can learn the essence of its value and the time and place where it can be realized.

3. Whenever we make any *One Thing Always the Most Important*, it's a sure bet that whatever else we forgot to give equal attention to will kick our ass.

4. Being able to make any something into "nothing," (for a brief time), has value. The value of *nothing* is that we can use it to build walls that allow detachment from a particular *here* so we can attach to something else *there*.

5. There is value to the carrot and value to the stick. Most of us may be influenced to act in certain ways based on punishments to avoid and rewards we seek to gain. The difficulty in predicting behavior here is that some of us will hate vegetables, and others like getting spanked. Some people's carrots are other people's sticks, and visa-versa. Some of us love solitude, and some of us think being alone is a special place in hell.

6. Valuing behavior as good/bad or right/wrong allows us to preserve the security of relationships. Valuing behavior as merely "different" allows us to preserve individual freedom. The conflict between these values provides a force for growth and balance.

7. Most values are simply tools that allow us to preserve our freedom to be secure in knowing who we are – and who we can become – alone and together.

8. Acting on general principles may be fine and noble, as long as they are yours. Most generals are never on the battlefield of life. It's we privates who fight the war.

9. If you value perfection, then remember that the best that we can become is perfectly human. This includes being perfectly confused, perfectly afraid, perfectly angry, perfectly sad, perfectly loving, perfectly mirthful, and in short, perfectly imperfect.

Human beings are primarily composed of water. If there is a basic essence to us all it would have to be called "awareness." In this we are more like water than we realize...

Responding to My Self

The *SELF* is this essence.

A being-having of...Behavior.
We are called many names, but of these, few are chosen by ourselves.
The self is like water, slipping through our fingers whenever we try to hold on to it. The basic elements of water are two atoms that, separated, are oxygen and hydrogen. Joined, they are water, H2O, a liquid. Something completely different. The configuration of Self is contained in the elements of "being" and "having." When we separate oxygen from hydrogen, we no longer get the compound of water. When we separate being from having, we no longer get a Self. When we join these elements, we get be-havior. If we attempt to treat these *individual* elements as if they were water, we are in deep trouble. If we attempt to use water as if it had the attributes of these

separate elements, we are also in for it.

Try diving into a pool of oxygen. Try breathing water. You see what I mean. The forms of water are liquid, ice, and vapor. These are all still "water." You might say that these forms are different ways that water responds to changes in the environment. In a sense, water is "aware," and changes its form in reaction to outside process. So we have forms of awareness as attributes of Self.

These forms of awareness are sensing, thinking, imagination and feeling. Be-havior. Being-having. Water takes the shape of the glass that contains it. On our planet, water is normally fluid. So is what we call the Self. When you start dealing with the fluid as if it were a solid, things get a bit messy. Water will flow out of any container that is not level. It will leak out of any container with holes in it. If water is left in an open glass at room temperature for any period of time, it will evaporate. (By evaporate I mean it will transform into another form).

The Self needs to be balanced, too. If we are not balanced, or channeled in an appropriate direction, our feelings begin to spill out all over the place. (We're just looking for an even level here).

We can freeze water. When we do, we can make it into a solid. We can heat water into vapor, which is now a gas. Liquid water, ice and steam can also exist simultaneously under certain conditions. It all depends on your environment. In all instances there are gains and concurrent losses of properties.

The Self has equal value in forms that are fluid, rigid, or diffuse.

When you are like ice, thoughts predominate. Sometimes the self may need to build a wall of ice to protect and preserve. Think of refrigerators. They keep things from getting spoiled. Thoughts/words act as our containers for experience. Yet, words are not enough to express the heat of our passions. It doesn't take much to melt most of us, (although some of us can get freeze dried and stay that way). But, ice is brittle, and can crack under enough pressure.

When you are steam, you can warm or burn. Here your imagination may allow you to float above the darkening clouds. But gases tend to expand indefinitely when released. They gradually spread themselves so thin that they disappear. Our dreams gradually disperse and fade unless we take action on them So do clouds – However, without clouds, life could not be sustained.

This form of water may be transitory, yet essential to our existence. When you are liquid you may flow with your feelings and heart. You touch all that contains you, and all that you are. But, as a liquid, you are forced to take on the shape of your environment, and flow with the pressure of any outside force that moves you.

You know when we say, *"Part of me feels this way"* or *"part of me wants this, or doesn't want this..."* we're really not talking about "parts." It's not your big toe, or stomach or sexual apparatus. We're talking about the ebb and flow of our needs and desires. The "sometimes" of our feelings – which are always changing. What may stay constant are our principles and integrity.

Who we want to be and become. The self is always both being and having...Awareness. Solid as ice, flowing gracefully as the heart and as ethereal as our dreams.

Acting like an "adult" is often confused with sexuality. The fact that our bodies develop and change plays only a small part in our maturity. Real adulthood is achieved in the growth of the mind and heart.

Small Change

Pretty/Handsome features...

Make one quarter of a man or woman. It's small change that most of us never earn. It was part of the genetic allowance from the parents. And, if we were really deprived, we can get it retail from the scalpers. A little nip here and tuck, and fold, and implant. The butterfly emerges from the cocoon of surgical gauze.

In truth, the wings are flimsy, and the beauty is often short lived. We eventually grow accustomed to the face and body of work, taking it for granted. Sexuality. To Re-Create. To Re-Produce. It's fun to be sexual and play with our bodies. Sometimes we make children, but most times it's for the hell and heaven of it. Sex is what most adults love best. It's what makes us adults – biologically. Just biologically – as I said, it's comparatively small change. To get your dollar's worth, you have to earn the other parts that make an adult. To re-create and re-produce something different than an orgasm. (Don't get me wrong here, orgasms are swell).

To re-create and re-produce another kind of being-having. To be really sexy, you need to be able to: re-create: a thought, a feeling and imagine. To think about your thoughts, and cherish them... You may discover the offspring of these encounters grow up to take care of you. Learn to feel what you are sensing, and to sense what you are feeling. It is important to define your self – to know what to call your thoughts, feelings, and attitudes. It is also important to know when you need to hold on to them, and when to let go with them, and when to do neither.

When you learn to pay attention to how you are paying attention to, it doesn't cost anything. Except, perhaps the loss of the illusions we can now see through. Large Change.

Imagine... that you can.

Think... that you will.

Feel... the unspoken.

Sense... the unknown.

Desire needs foresight to become intent... your will and you had best make a pact.

Will and I

Will and I were not always good friends. At first, he was headstrong. In other words, he was a total, and I mean totally, selfish baby – I don't mean selfish all the time. When he was satisfied with himself, after a nice warm meal, after some cuddling, he was all smiles. But, if he was hungry for something, stand back. At first he would cry with rage. Then he'd stamp his feet. He made demands as if he were the king of the universe.

I told him that if he was going to play king, there were reciprocal duties involved. A king also had to take care of his subjects. You know, raise the army to defend against the foreign invaders, help the poor, make sure there was enough food for the population, maintain the roads, fix the sewers, etc.. Then, I said, then the king can be a taxing son-of-a-bitch like you.

As we grew together, I was sometimes separated from Will. Others took over, and I learned at times I had to do without. Of course you do. You can't always be hanging out together. I had to learn from other people as well as through my self. I must admit, I also pushed my Will away, even down. I let other people pull me. After all, they were so much bigger and smarter than me and my Will.

You see, I was looking out for the future. If I was going to be like them, I had to hang out with them. That meant leaving Will behind. Almost completely.

Except when I was alone. When these others left, or maybe I got away, or both…it didn't matter who I was like. I didn't like me. How could I? – I learned a lot of stuff, sure. So what. I got smart like them, and big like them, and now, what the hell was I supposed to do? So I allowed my very own Will back into my life.

At first, completely again. We ran into a lot of trouble that way, alienating the new people in my life, but losing some of them was no big deal. But the ones I guess that loved me, or cared for me, clued me in. They told me about the king bit. Now Will and I are good friends. I trust him – not always – but in the important things. I indulge him as long as it isn't harmful to me or anybody else. In return, he helps me rule over the kingdom I run. He's there when I really need him, lending some extra muscle, or brainstorming with me when I've got a problem. He reminds me when it's time to take care of my own ass just as he reminds me when to move it. I still give him time off for good behavior. Sometimes he's wild, sometimes hard as steel, sometimes he is a legacy. Most of all, we've become good friends. My will and I.

We can never "have" our ideals, other than as memories or fantasies What we can do is "be" them.

Ideally...

Sometimes we confuse the outside with the inside. This is especially true for what we call our "ideals." Someone may act or perform in a way that mirrors perfection. We think, "how…intelligent, artistic, compassionate, courageous, virtuous, honorable, graceful…" These are the actions that give us both meaning and purpose. These are our values personified into deeds. Our heroes manifest these ideals. We strive to enact them in our lives. We often daydream of performing in these ways, or carry memories of past victories. One quality that these ideals have in common is that they are seen as the best that one can do. You don't have to feel the best to *be* the best – Hell, you can even *feel* the best and totally screw things up. We create strife for ourselves in believing that one day we will "have," or "own" these ideals. We can't. We don't always subjectively experience ideals – we don't always feel them inside. Just the same, we can *be* these behaviors in our actions.

Most of you have seen or read *The Wizard of Oz.* Remember? Dorothy, Toto, the Scarecrow, the Tin Man, the Cowardly Lion? Yeah, you remember. The Scarecrow wanted a brain. The Tin Man wanted a heart. The Lion wanted courage. And they got them, right? Well, yes and no. The Scarecrow got a diploma, the Tin Man got a heart-shaped clock, and the Lion got a medal. Because the ideals of intelligence, compassion and courage are not things to *have*, they're behaviors we *enact*. One can't feel courage. Being brave means being scared shitless and doing it anyway. The practiced diver who does a triple somersault off the high dive may feel cocky, or arrogant, or numb. It's the little kid jumping off for the first time we describe as "brave." We can think we've flunked a test and later discover we got an "A." We can give a homeless person our spare change, if only to get them to leave us the hell alone. In all the above instances we may not have felt or thought we were intelligent, compassionate or courageous. Whenever I'm acting "virtuous" you can bet your ass that inside I'm feeling lustful, greedy, envious and lazy...and very, very frustrated. There is no virtue without temptation.

To be confident also means to be certain. We frequently apply this certainty to our capabilities. We also need to be confident about our limitations. We need to be sure about what we can't and won't do. To accept these limits allows us continue to make the best efforts that we can where we are capable. We need to be confident that we don't know everything there is to know. About ourselves, about others, about the universe we live in. Although this limitation may constrict our ego and feelings of control, at the same time it expands our heart with the gift of hope. So, if you think you have to "feel" virtuous, intelligent, compassionate or noble prior to any undertaking, think again. You may be avoiding the task at hand. We have the necessity of being, at times, uncertain and confused. Otherwise, how can we ever discover anything new? We never truly know what another feels. To know in this sense would imply being that person. At best we can identify with...When we accomplish this task, we have built a bridge of belonging. We are separate still, yet now with the right to choose...Ideally. One for all; all for one.

Here are some ways to consider the struggle for being "good"...

Guidelines to Courage and Virtue

1. All ideals are patterns of behavior that we fool ourselves into believing we can "have." We can't *have* ideal behavior, although we can *enact* this behavior. (Sometimes with no clue that we've even done the right thing).

2. The reasons for this paradox are the external descriptions of ideal behavior rarely match our internal feelings while in the process.

3. In order for someone to be courageous, they must also be

frightened silly, acting despite their fear. Fear is a prerequisite to courage. Those who know no fear are either too ignorant to know any better, or suffering from the blindness of an inflated ego that obstructs their vision and hearing.

4. In order for someone to act "virtuous," they must also feel lustful, lazy, envious, slothful, piggish, spiteful, and greedy. A person with virtue doesn't do just what feels good – they do what does good.

5. Most of us who refuse to act with virtue and courage only stop ourselves because we are unwilling to admit that we have normal human fears and human desires. We forget that the acceptance and recognition of our defects is the first step in changing them.

6. The way to develop most personal strengths involves both exposure to pain and tolerance to frustration.

7. This is why, whenever we pray for patience, God, Fate, or the Universe at Large will put us into a major traffic jam. Whenever we pray for courage, something even more terrifying comes to scare us. (If you pray for unconditional love, there is a good chance that you will be crucified).

8. Praying for the welfare of others may be your safest bet if you have a tendency towards laziness. Remember though – all virtues may be bastardized into the service of the ego to prove that you're better than those other immoral jerks.

10. You aren't, especially when you brag about how humble you really are. If you are more than fair you are being unfair to yourself; if you are loyal to the treacherous you are only asking for more betrayal.

11. All virtues may become vices if we blindly act without

considering the effect they have on both others and ourselves. Faith, Hope, and Charity are wonderful qualities when properly invested. However, they never helped anyone in farming the Sahara desert.

Responsibility is only a burden when we carry it because we're afraid of our freedom...

Tips for Sailing

There was once this guy who loved to sail. It made him feel free. Now, sailing can be like flying across the surface of the water. The ocean's spray blows across your face as you feel the hum of your craft gliding and racing. It's a wonderful feeling.

So one day our friend is anchored out in the sea, just catching some rays. It's time for him to go, and he tries to pull the anchor up. But it's stuck. It's too deep to dive for it, and he works for a while trying to dislodge it. Finally, very frustrated, he cuts it loose. He's having a good ole' time sailing back until a storm hits him. Without the anchor to steady him, he's dead meat. His boat gets hit by a gnarly wave, tips, takes in water and starts to go down. He barely makes it back to shore alive. He knew he shouldn't have let go. So the sailor makes a vow – never to let go of that anchor again. On his new ship, he sets sail and people often stop and laugh. 'Cause he's sweating and straining as he carries that anchor right on his back.

Sailing isn't much fun for him anymore. Most ships carry an anchor. An anchor provides stability, holding our ship in place. When we need to take in provisions and deliver goods we use the anchor to insure that we don't drift. When we're out at sea and a storm overtakes us, we drop anchor and face the winds head-on, riding through the waves from a steadfast position. Responsibility is also an anchor. It fixes our position relative to other persons and harbors of security. We become stable as we take on responsibilities for and to others.

The anchor is only useful if we can also sail our vessel. It does very little good to load up all the goods and be unable to travel. To be responsible, to be able to respond, means that we learn to use the weight in a manner that helps us in our journey. If the weight stops us from sailing, then it is useless.

There are a few typical ways that we make ourselves flounder or capsize. One is to set sail with your anchor down. Here you can wind up going in circles. If you have an extremely long chain or rope attached to your anchor, your circles get a little wider. People who sail with their anchors down may not really want to face winds and waves of change. They need that fixed position.

Once you have discovered this mistake, you can make the second mistake. You can cut your anchor loose. You are now free to sail. But you can bet your ass that sooner or later you'll need supplies or a storm will come in. Either way, you're going to run aground or sink. After this occurs, you're going to need a new ship. A lot of folks who have had this experience now get terrified. They realize the anchor was their security and swear to turn over a new leaf.

These are the guys who start carrying their anchors on their backs. Makes them feel pretty safe – and very miserable. There is only so much we can carry for so long. Regardless of how strong our back is. No matter how muscular our shoulders are. We have to put that anchor down. Here, a fortunate few learn the most helpful way to use the anchor. They see another difference besides letting go and holding on. They don't put the anchor down – they put it aside. They realize that having something within your reach may be (at times) more useful than throwing it overboard or clinging to it. If we must carry it *always,* then it gradually weakens us. If we *never* have it we will eventually sink. It can surprise you to realize that the vessel is carrying both your weight and the weight of the anchor, anyway. At that point we will see that the anchor is both heavy and light. It all depends on how you use it.

A responsibility doesn't disappear when you put it aside. Nor should it. We need to anchor. We also need to sail.

Guilt may help us maintain a certain structure or boundary for our lives. The thing to consider here is who and what gets to live within that framework...

Borders and Boarders

Guilt is feeling and thoughts. It's this sense of "wrongness" that tightens our gut. This feeling may be accompanied with images of punishment, loss and deprivation. Guilt is a lot like punching a hole through your wall. When we feel guilty, we have crossed a certain boundary. That boundary is a limit that gives us security. It is a wall in our home, or the fence that marks the territory that we identify as ours. We don't want anyone to mess with it, including ourselves. We feel guilt whenever we do something that changes that border, whether we're really "being bad" or not.

Maybe you knocked that hole in the wall because you're adding a room. Maybe you are doing it because you are angry. Either way, the boundary we once had is going to look pretty ragged. If we knock the wall down because we are remodeling, well, it's still going to look just as bad as if we had a major tantrum.

Friends and family may complain about the state of affairs in either instance. The only difference between the between the two is that when we are remodeling we use the plans, tools, and time for making a new border. (I hope you also informed those people you live with before you start). Our borders outside help us to protect ourselves and live in comfort. They are defenses against those who would abuse or neglect us. We give friends the keys to our doors and gates. We give those we love the combinations to what we have locked inside. Every outside border or wall also has an inside support to keep it in good standing. Inside, most of us have a wall between who we think we are and who we are afraid to become.

DON'T feel think imagine behave like THAT!

All well and good if we are choosing these rules for ourselves. Not so hot if someone shoved them down our throat. If we were forced to swallow this as a type of support, we need to examine the lease we have on life, and the nature of our walls. We have this saying, "Let your conscience be your guide." Well, a guide works for you.

A guide gives direction, leads you in a safe way, and still gets you where *you want* to go. A guide doesn't spend their time telling you how bad, stupid, or incompetent you are. (Such borders need to change. They support walls that have been used to keep us trapped).

Face it. – Change of any kind can make us feel anxious and guilty. Your place is going to look a mess, and it'll take a while to get things right. Shitty thoughts are going to nag and bitch at you they whisper to you that they'll never leave, and you can't make them. Complementing each criticism you receive speeds up the process of movement. You know, like "thank you for taking the time to be concerned," or "You are really watching out for my welfare, thanks." If you have no walls, no one place will be your home. This is scary for most of us. Some think that this is the ultimate goal. They believe this means that every place should be their home. Just do me a favor, if you are one of them. Check with me before you try to move into my place.

It might be advisable to chart this territory prior to calling your travel agent to book that guilt trip…

Guidelines For Guilt

1. Guilt is a feeling we experience when we ignore or break values that secure our relationship with others and our own self-image. Guilt serves as a wall that shelters the building of our identity. When we break down these barriers we may feel both guilty and anxious.

2. Thoughts related to the feeling of guilt will label self as bad,

wrong, evil, immoral, impure, dirty, or some other kind of screw-up.

3. Guilt functions to maintain consistent behaviors. The beliefs and attitudes that support this consistency come from personal experience, family interaction, and culture. Behaviors that we call "good" are positively valued for preserving our security. Behaviors that we learn to call "bad" are negatively valued for disrupting our security.

4. We can learn to feel guilty about any behavior at all, depending on our teachers and environment. We can learn to feel guilty about caring for others. We can learn to feel guilty about caring for ourselves. Guilt can taint any emotion, idea, fantasy, perception, or action.

5. If there was extreme neglect in our childhood we may feel guilt when we are successful and independent. If there was abuse we may feel guilty when we are vulnerable or assertive. If we were both abused and neglected we will call our travel agent to book guilt trips for every occasion.

6. Guilt can be categorized into two distinct types, true guilt and false guilt.

7. True guilt occurs when we have broken values and limits that *we have chosen for ourselves.* The violation of these principles leads to actions that exploit or diminish the welfare of self and/or others.

8. False guilt occurs when we have broken values and limits that we have blindly followed. Guilt emerges here even without exploiting and diminishing the welfare and genuine capability of others.

9. False guilt usually includes thoughts, feelings, and fantasies that are reactions to change. True guilt includes the awareness that we made a deliberate conscious choice that directly or indirectly harms another.

10. There are no immoral feelings; there are only immoral actions. Any thought that emerges as a reaction is not immoral either, unless we intend to willfully use it for harm and selfish gain.

11. The resolution for true guilt includes the following actions:
    a. Acknowledging to the other we have exploited or diminished that our actions have caused harm.
    b. Making a commitment that we will not repeat these actions. (And consistently following this vow).
    c. Making just and fair reparations for the damage we have caused. Just and fair are to be mutually decided on by you and the other. A neutral Third party you both agree to may also be helpful here in case of stalemates.
    d. If, for whatever reason, we continue to betray or harm, we must end that relationship in order to protect the other from ourselves.

12. The resolution for false guilt includes the following actions:
    a. An acknowledgment to our self that we are allowing a value, belief, or idea to diminish and exploit what are otherwise good intentions. (These good intentions relate to maintaining our own security and freedom in relationships).
    b. Explore the origin of these values, and identifying with whom, when, where and how we were taught these rules. We need to examine our current relationships and identify who else may be invested in keeping our false guilt. We can explore our fantasies of gain and loss that may occur when we transform these values. Exploring can be done in writing and with a trusted friend.
    c. Decide on alternate values that help maintain security and also allow for healthy self-expression, qualified risk taking, and personal freedom.
    d. Confront both our original teachers and others who support values that undermine our worth. Our feelings may include

anger and resentment. These must be expressed without shaming and guilt-tripping the other – without putting oneself in physical or material danger. This process is not about finding fault or blame; it is concerned with accountability and change. This means holding others responsible for their behavior while holding yourself accountable for your own.

e. Define concrete behaviors (spelling them out if necessary) that are desired from these persons in question. We may need to determine if the other is even capable of allowing or making a change.

f. Set and follow through with consistent consequences for others should they continue to provoke false guilt. The most useful consequences involve distancing or disengaging in some way from that relationship. This can include anything from hanging up in the middle of a telephone conversation to ending a friendship.

g. Set and follow through with rewards and validation for the other when they succeed in changing. These rewards should be based on the other's needs and wants, provided they don't jeopardize your welfare or integrity.

h. Should you fail to carry these actions out, false guilt will persist.

You will probably continue to live below your true potential for success and happiness, and seem to have a good excuse for it, as "they" are keeping you down. Procrastination is one form of guilt. Get moving on this stuff. *Now.*

Human reptiles can be very warm – until you decide the sun doesn't rise or set on them...

Cold Blooded

When we call someone "cold blooded" we usually mean that they are uncaring, unfeeling, selfish and self-centered – A "snake." In other words, A Reptile.

Well, that's not what being cold blooded is really about. A warm-blooded animal has a consistent internal temperature. We humans tend to stay at around 98.6 degrees – reptiles are another story. Their internal temperatures vary with the climate. If it's 100 degrees, the reptile is going to be 100 degrees. If it's 20 below zero, the reptile is going to be 20 below zero. Reptiles can be hot-blooded too. Or, in extreme temperature, most likely dead. Reptiles can only survive in a limited range. Supposedly, mammals evolved from reptiles. Becoming warm blooded allowed us to adapt with the changing conditions on the planet.

Now that you understand this process a little better, you can see that "cold blooded" reptile can have both hot blood and cold blood. It all depends on the temperature of the environment. So now let me tell you about human reptiles.

Human reptiles are those who pretend to feel what others in their environment feel. Human reptiles are those pretend to think what others in their environment think. They sense what others in their environment sense. Being cold-blooded can prove difficult for those in positions of authority relative to others in the environment. If I have to be exactly like you every time you are in fear, pain, and anger, we're both in deep trouble. The doctors doing the operations would have to cut themselves every time they perform surgery. The parents attempting to comfort screaming children would have to do so screaming with their own fear.

Okay, I know I'm exaggerating. It is important to be able to accept and to show your acceptance of what someone else is experiencing. If we are dealing with another's anger, fear, or pain and we immerse ourselves in their feelings, then both of us will be lost. Some people mistakenly call this former process "empathy." Don't let yourself be fooled. It isn't. If you are going to be empathic towards another, you can imagine how they feel, think, and sense. And you will do this while you still feel and think exactly as yourself. Both are added *together* to create empathy. It's not being able to put on both their shoes, just one of them. Keep on one of your own.

Reptiles always have their own agenda, no matter what they pretend. For a chameleon, the pretense of relating is camouflage. They "love" you as long as you're doing exactly what they want. They can appear caring and passionate. Until you want to do something different. Then, they'll hiss and drip venom. In order to accomplish this empathy thing you need to be a mammal. That means your internal temperature has to be consistent. You're still going to feel the changes in the environment around you, and you're still going to get cold, and you're still going to get hot. If you're not careful you can be overwhelmed if the environment is too extreme at either end.

What keeps us consistent internally is our values, or principles. This is something reptiles lack. Oh, they can talk a good game, but look at their actions. Perhaps your values are the Ten Commandments, or the twelve steps, or the seven paths, or the Constitution, or whatever beliefs that have worked for you. Following these guidelines gives us the security of knowing who we are. However, they only really work if we have digested them. This means that they can't really be of any use to you unless they have been chewed over, broken down, and absorbed into the body of our minds and hearts. Swallowing them whole doesn't work, except for giving us gas and heartburn.

You digest a principle by using it in your actions and experiencing its effects upon yourself. Like it or not, you will eventually become warm blooded. The reptiles will eventually sense that you are not one of them and probably show their fangs. If there's a pack of them around you, I'd recommend that you give them a cold shoulder. They hate icy climates the most. They can't help it, so don't even bother trying to blame them. If any of them are interested in evolution, use some empathy. Or change the topic to music. Even snakes can be charmed if you know how to play their song.

The universe of space-time is curved. Every straight line is a circle in disguise, with endings and beginnings at the same point...

In Steadness

There really isn't such a thing as stopping, you know. Stopping is an illusion. Think about it. We're all flying through the universe at 25,000 miles per second. Even when you are driving your car, and you use the brake, do you stop your car? Hell no. You *start* to downshift; you *start* to take your foot off the gas and clutch. You *start* to put pressure on the break pedal. When your car, (which is hopefully still running,) comes to this particular place you want it to be, you *start* looking, or you *start* fiddling with the radio, or you *start doing* something else. When the movie's ended, don't you *start* to get up? Most of us run into the problem of trying to "stop" a particular way of thinking, or feeling, or acting, or imagining. Most of us fail at this task. You see, it doesn't matter if you get someone to "stop." People can always appear to stop. They can say they are stopping even as they run you over. It only matters what you get yourself or someone else to *start*. Instead.

You can't walk away from any place unless you are also walking toward a different place. Instead. So, if you appear to be stuck in your thoughts, thinking even more about it is rarely a solution. Unless you keep loading on thoughts until you are so overwhelmed that you do get to take a nervous breakdown. Unfortunately, although this did relieve the camel, the procedure also broke its back. Avoid trying to stop the thoughts. Focus on your imagination or your senses. The senses and the imagination are two separate bridges you can take. The ultimate destination here may be to get in touch with your feelings. To leave "here," we must start to follow or make the path of Instead. It allows us to arrive "there." To *check out* of your mind, *check into* your body, or into imagining where you would like to be. If you would like to change, remember changes start as small seeds that grow with consistent attention and care.

If you appear to be stuck in your feelings, don't try to stop them, either. You can use the same bridges in reverse. If feelings are overwhelming, check into your senses. See, hear, and touch what is outside of you here and now. Another way is to use real wood. A piece of paper and pen will do nicely. Start to write about what you experiences. As you write, you will begin to notice a change. You have already changed. You are writing, instead of moaning or ranting.

So, – *In steadness,* – a wonderful tool. But just a tool. These are not the ultimate solutions to end all suffering, or The Way To Change Your Life Completely In The Privacy Of Your Own Home At Only Minutes Per Day At No Cost At All To You. You are going to need to take some other actions as well. This is just a start. – Instead.

HERE and NOW is the only time and place where choice is possible. So, where and when are YOU?

Choice and Security

You know, "always" and "never" have a lot in common. After all, if something never happens, then it *always* never happens. Any *"never"* is an *"always"* in disguise. Most of us define time as a before-during- after experience. Always and never are used to describe the totality of this. Before was our past, during is our present, and after will be our future. Always/never includes the whole package we use for predicting security.

So we think. What if time doesn't really work this way? What if, as the physicists and mystics tell us, there is something different? The only time you can make a choice is *Now*. We can make choices *Now* for the future time of *Then*. It's funny how when that particular future emerges, *our choice is transformed into a have-to/must/ should.* (We *chose* to go to the beach on the weekend. On Saturday, we *had* to go because we planned it).

Our designs and plans to preserve freedom wind up trapping us.

Mainly because it wasn't freedom we were after in the first place. It was security. When we hold onto our security, simultaneously we let go of our capability to choose. When we hold on to our freedom, we simultaneously let go of our security. It's like work and play. It's like time and space. We hold onto space when we hold onto security. Space includes material objects we acquire and roles we adopt. We can make an object out of anything. A lover, a car, a home, the esteem of our friends. All these can be viewed as objects that must be *"had."* So we make these plans and designs to *have and keep.*

To accomplish this, we take on a role, usually that of a "good" worker, friend, spouse, parent. We become responsible. As we attempt to grasp and maintain these objectives, our hands are full. Our eyes are fixed on the map again. We let it dictate, instead of guide. As we do, there is little, if any time to make choices, or to enjoy the security we have obtained.

On the other extreme, we may realize the futility of this kind of existence. We may refuse to commit ourselves to any certain order or structure. We become as free as the wind. Now we have all the time in the world to make choices. Yet, we may have given up the objects or roles we need to be free *with.* Here we become like the child who refuses to clean their room, as they have better things to do. Such as playing baseball. Except, now we can't find the glove to play with. It's lost in the disorder we refuse to order. I don't really know if this is any "better" than the child who knows where their glove is, and is too busy straightening and cleaning to make time for play. Choice and freedom are present provided that we are aware of this here and now. Allow the space for times of choice. Security is present when we are aware of the next there and then. Make the time for a secure space.

Part of knowing who you are is knowing what you like...

Favorite Things and Activities Inventory

Describe your most "perfect day."

Do you have a favorite aunt, uncle brother/sister, cousin or grandparent? Why are they the favorite?

B) FOOD and DINING

Name your top three in the following categories

favorite main courses:
favorite vegetables:
favorite beverages:
favorite ice creams, cakes, pies or other deserts:

What are your favorite snack foods?

What are your favorite restaurants?

Does you like to cook? If so, what?

How about dinner parties or dining out with friends?

C) DRESS and FASHION

What are the brand names you like to wear?

Where do you like to shop for clothes? Name the top three stores.

What are your favorite colors to wear?

Do you like jewelry? What kind? How about other stuff, like belts or handbags. What kind?

D) ENTERTAINMENT
(These are more passive activities where we sit back and enjoy watching or listening)

What are your favorite television shows, if any?

What are your favorite kinds of film?

Name the top three actors and actresses you like.

Do you like any sports? If so, what are your favorite teams?

Do you have any favorite types of books? If so, who are your favorite authors?

Do you have a favorite magazine?

What are your favorite types of music?

Name your favorite band, singer or orchestra

Do you have a favorite musical instrument?

What kind of art does you like? Are there any artists whose works you admire? Painting, sculpture and all kinds of art can be included here. Do you like to go to galleries or exhibits?

What about plays and musical theater?

Any other things you like to go to, museums, rodeos, the circus, you name it.

E) HOBBIES and ACTIVITIES

These are things we're active participants in...

What do you like to do to just have fun?

What are your hobbies? This includes anything from collecting to making stuff..

Do you like to play any sports? If so, what are they or were they?

Are there any sports, exercise or physical activities you enjoy doing with others ?

Do you like board games or card games? If so, what do you like to play?

If you were to take some classes just for fun, what would they be?

Do you like to dance? If so, what kind of dancing?

What kind of other creative pursuits might interest you? (stuff like writing, acting, art, crafts, singing, carpentry, clothing design, car repair, you name it...

F) CARING and AFFECTION
How would you like others to express their affection for you? With words, phrases or pet names?

With touch?

Identify FIFTEEN CARING ACTIONS you could do for yourself on a daily, weekly, or even just a few times a month that would make you feel loved and validated:
1.

2.

3.

4.

5.

6.

7.

8.

9.

10.

11.

12.

13.

14.

15.

G) SEX and ROMANCE

How do you know a partner wants to make love with you? What do they do or say that indicates they are in the mood?

What are the romantic behaviors they did (or used to do) that made you feel close and desire them?

What are the sensual behaviors they did that made you feel aroused?

Do you like the lights on or off? Do you like candles?

Do you like to talk while making love, or prefer it to be quiet? If you like to hear them talk, what turns them on?

How do you like to be kissed? Where do you like to be kissed?

How do you like to be touched? Where do you like to be touched during foreplay? At climax? After?

Do they have any special fantasies of what you'd like to be able to do with them, or what they could do to you?

H) TRUST and RESPECT

What do you consider your five top strengths of character?
a)
b)
c)
d)
e)

Name an instance when you last acted:
with self respect

with compassion

with faith

with trust

with strength or assertion

with humility

with grace

with patience

with courage

By the way…you could try this out with your partner and see what you can discover as well.

Balance requires time. And time is quite a different commodity when you learn how it really works…

The Middle Ground

It's about balance. You know. Finding the middle ground. The center. The harmony. We have other words for this too. Justice, fairness, equity. We all at least pretend to support these values. Some of us actually believe in them. I do.

It's still hard as hell to balance the equation in our actions. And, I think it's because we get confused on what the middle ground is. The middle ground is easy to find in Space.

Take any line. We start at Point a on one side, going to (let's call it point c) on the other side.

a._____.c

We can pick out the midpoint with a fair degree of accuracy. We'll call that point b.

a._____.b_____.c

As easy as A-B-C. Right? B is that middle ground. *In Space*. But we live in *both* space and time. When you attempt to find the midpoint of a line in space, the midpoint appears to come before the end point. Let's add another dimension. What we'll do here is scale our line in the dimension of time. This means we draw a picture of *how* the line was drawn in the first place, and when each point was made. The *When* of the line.

We have the same beginning point a.

a._____.

We next went all the way to the other side *before* we got to the midpoint. So, let's call this other point b.

a._____.b

Our movement in time *was completed at the midpoint of the line*, which we can call c.

We had to backtrack to get there.

a._____.c_____.b
      <.................

It's pretty weird when you really think about it. The midpoint in space comes before the end point The midpoint in time comes after the end point. Remember the theme to *The Twilight Zone*?

You see, we don't just live in spatial dimensions. We also live in the dimension of time. As a matter of fact, space and time are inseparable companions. Time is a dimension of movement and motion. It is all of the *NOWS* any space can manifest. In time, an oak tree can be an acorn, a seedling, a tree, a chair, or even a warm fire. We perceive these objects as different "things." They are all aspects of an oak tree. Different branches growing from the same trunk. Which brings me back to balance, middle grounds, and harmony.

You have to go from the beginning to the end before you really know what the middle is. Halfway there doesn't cut it. You can't know what's halfway unless you've been to the other side. It's just another end until you go back over some of the ground you've gained. We tend to view all human behavior in pairs of opposites. (It's called dialectics) Selfish/selfless, weak/strong, stupid/intelligent, unimaginative/ creative, cold/warm. The list is endless. All of us seem to load these traits with a good/bad, or desirable/undesirable value. We aspire to reach the goal of being caring, strong, smart, imaginative and feeling individuals. How is it that we become caretakers who enable others to become greedy and exploit us? How is it that we go to college and adopt a narrow focus that dulls our vision? How is it that we exercise to the point of ruining our bodies? How is it that we become so imaginative that our big picture is so big that we can't even get it on canvass?

How is it that we lose our warmth of caring after being burned so often? Because we lose our balance. We forget the middle ground. Our goal, our end point in time, requires a balance. It can be very smart to admit when you are being stupid. It can be very strong to admit when you are being weak. It can be very caring of you to be cold to another, especially when their dependency on you keeps them stuck.

The endpoint in time means that you are attached to both sides equally. Otherwise, we end up where we started from in the first place. Only the unintelligent outsmart themselves. Only the unimaginative live in the ruts of passive contemplation without action. It is those of us who stuff our anger who are most likely to explode. The harder we try not to be something, the easier it is to become what you are trying to avoid. It is those of us who wish to prove our strength who take on such burdens that ultimately make us helpless.

Mainly because we get confused about that end point. It just seems to be on the other side. If you wish to perform like clockwork remember that clocks go around in circles, and that time doesn't ever stop. It just changes the shape of things. That the pendulum swings back and forth to keep that clock working. That everything is manifested in time. And that the end point is somewhere in the middle ground.

"Pathologizing" means that you are defining a condition as "sick." Well, mental illness depends more on context than anything else...

A Reasonable Doubt

Justice is first a matter of belief. In the United States any alleged "criminal" is innocent until proven guilty. The proof must leave no reasonable doubt in the minds of the jurors. If there is a reasonable doubt, a verdict of guilty is dismissed. We could have gone the other way. Some countries do. Our laws could be geared to prove innocence. If this were the case, then the burden of proof would rest on the accused. Innocence would have to be established beyond a reasonable doubt. (The media in our country often uses this tactic with political figures and movie stars. You can see how *fair* it is).

Our legal system reflects a deeper set of values. If we are innocent, then we are "good." If we are guilty, then we are "bad." I believe our framework of law is based on the assumption that human beings are essentially good, and so "badness" must be proven. In psychology we also have a set of values that have this good-bad association. We say that behavior is either "sick" or "healthy." Healthy is "good" and sick is "bad." The difference between the legal and medical models is simple. While the courts presume innocence, we shrink types presume sickness. After all, if the person who engages our services isn't sick, there is really no reason to charge them money to "treat" them. We are trained to look for what is wrong, what is dysfunctional, what, in essence, is "bad."

There's another way to see things – if you look hard enough. There is this guy who comes to see me. He is a married, middle-aged man. He's nervous. Everybody is when they first see a shrink. I thank him for being so nervous as it makes it easier for me to at least look as if I know what I'm doing. He laughs. I do my usual introduction to the world of psychology bit, establish myself as an authority and all. But mainly I listen and look, feel and imagine. He's telling me about his obsession with sex. He's a voyeur. He likes to listen and look too. At the "dirty" stuff. He's no Peeping Tom, mind you. He doesn't buy magazines or videos. He uses the television, or ordinary magazines. He looks for the obscene word, the bit of exposed breast, naked bottoms. Even as he does, he is filled with guilt. He has already judged himself as a sick pervert.

He is satisfied with his marriage. With further probing from me, it appears that he has a normal, satisfactory sexual relationship with his wife. So you may wonder what I do. I could explore the past with him, and find out where he was made "sick" through some trauma imposed by the authority of parental or religious discipline. Probably take about two years. I could get a new car out of it. But I presume innocence and health.

So instead, we find a time and place where this behavior has value. That was the first and last time I saw him. He is now busy with his new job. I couldn't think of a more qualified man for the role. All day long he looks and listens for obscene words, gestures, and nakedness. He is very good at his work, and very proud of his position. He became a censor for one of the television networks. We agreed that it was a dirty job, but someone has to do it. For the record, I believe that all my clients are healthy until proven sick. Most of the proof comes from their parents, spouses, agents from the court, or other members of my profession. Me? I take all of this into account… But I have this reasonable doubt about all the dirt we dish out. As you will soon see…

Speaking of bad raps, sex and dirt are often much maligned. Dirt is the more innocent party…

Good Clean Dirt

You know, it never ceases to amaze me how we are so prejudiced about dirt. For example, "You dirty, filthy, nasty… so and so." Now, I'm not saying that whoever or whatever you are so upset about doesn't aggravate you. Oh, those of you with open wounds – I can see your point. You could get infected and all but think about it. You have a right to your feelings. What I am saying is that dirt doesn't deserve this comparison. This verbal abuse toward innocent dirt. Really now. We couldn't live without dirt. Dirt grows all of our crops. Dirt is responsible for all of our animal life. Without dirt you would not be alive at all. With dirt there are flowers, and food, and the fresh smells of growing life.

Yet, most of you insist on defining whatever offends your moral sense as "dirty." I suppose that you would like to consider yourselves clean as the driven snow, as in Snow White. Now, I like snow as much as the next guy. But life doesn't grow much in the snow. We don't harvest in the wintertime. Life slows down; animals hibernate and live off the fat that they've stored. The coldness of our thoughts works to preserve us in much the same way. When we are cold, life slows down, and so does the decay that goes hand in hand with life. When we start to warm up again, we begin a season of growing. Decay must also begin now. Life and death are secret partners. The decay brings us back to dirt.

Ashes to ashes, dust to dust. Dirt, which really brings us back to life. When most people use the word "dirty" as an adjective, you know what they are usually talking about. Sex. Yep. Fornication, intercourse, petting, masturbation, fucking, screwing, and so on. Things change and grow when you are involved in these "dirty" activities. We sow the seeds of life here (or at the very least, we are practicing farmers of the future). In the winter, we put our plows away, and leave the land untouched. Unless, of course you live in California, Florida, or other non-temperate zones where those decadent people have the nerve to grow things that feed us all year long. They have a lot of good clean dirt in these places.

The organs that we use to be sexual with are the same organs we use for eliminating body wastes. These wastes provide the essential ingredients that help flowers, trees, crops, and all life flourishes. All shit makes good fertilizer. The problem is, the fertilizer is only useful in the garden. Supposedly, we got kicked out of the Garden a long,

long time ago. In that Garden, there was no shame, and I assume that we saw the dirt for exactly what it was. A source of life. So, perhaps we'd best make a new garden.

To accomplish this task will require a warmer climate. Not all of us were meant to be farmers. All of us, however, reap the benefits of what the farmers produce. All of us take from the earth, and all of us now live and survive because of everything that you have frozen into your minds as dirt. If you have difficulty with your sexuality, there are ways to defrost. Think of a puppy or kitten. They get dirty, too. She or he will jump right up on your lap, just wanting to be touched, and petted. They can't help themselves. It's natural, innocent and playful. You feel the warmth of the fur, and the silkiness, and the smooth firm muscles underneath. They move with every stroke of your hand, wanting the attention and affection. You can't help yourself, either. What could be more innocent, and sweet, and warm, and wonderful? So when it's safe for you, in all the ways you need it to be. When you can make the time, and are of the inclination, get down and play. In the good, clean, dirt.

Making a God of Freedom OR Security has an unfortunate effect.

Artful Dodges

There are these two artists I know...

One used to paint on canvas. However, as his talent grew he felt limited by that space. He worried that if he got an inspiration to extend beyond the piece his creativity would be stilted. So he switched to painting on walls. This worked well for a while. But one day, at the top of a wall he got this image that he couldn't complete. Because the wall stopped. He hasn't painted since that day. He's been trapped by his need for freedom.

The second artist says that canvas is the only way to go. He selects three feet by three feet pieces. But they have to be stretched perfectly, and positioned perfectly, with the perfect kind of lighting, with the perfect type of stand. He hasn't painted anything for years either. He still working on setting up his easel. He's been trapped by his need for structure. By security.

When I think of them both I paint this picture in my mind. I see an eagle soaring in the sky and I think of freedom. Then I look closely and see that the eagle has no feet. No talons to attack or defend. No way to land, or rest, or build a nest. Then a second image emerges. I see the eagle with these powerfully muscled legs. The talons are sharp and strong and nimble. But the wings are clipped.

There is no freedom without structure. There is no structure without freedom.

Here's another non-linear way to think. Curve balls are some of the best pitches to have...

Guidelines for Problem Solving

Step 1.
Accept that everything is happening for just the reasons you think. What you perceive as a problem is a problem. Proceed on the usual course of action. In the event of failure, go on.

Step 2.
Accept that everything that you think about the situation or event is exactly the opposite of what you presumed. What you perceive as a problem is also a solution. What are the hidden benefits that this problem produces for you and others involved? All shit does make good fertilizer. Consider finding the garden that is being nurtured here. If no garden exists, at least move the crap from the living room. In the event of failure, go to Step 3.

Step 3.
Add your initial and secondary assumptions about the situation together. This new perspective will be neither the same as, nor the

opposite of your previous beliefs. Proceed with the awareness that you may not be able to make an impact relative to the problem and solution until you perceive it as something completely different. Now take action. In the event of failure, go to Step 4.

Step 4.
Consider that you are involved in this mess to avoid dealing with other issues you are afraid of facing. It just may be that the best you can do here is to choose to admit your limitations, ask for help, and quit being so damn stubborn.

Most of us think in "EITHER OR" terms. Thinking in "EITHER-AND" has its own merits...

On One Hand

Okay. Now, pay attention. (I don't know why we use the word "pay" here. Attention doesn't really cost anything and time isn't always money). Extend your right hand and hold it open. Good.

So, what are you holding on to? Nothing? Nope. Nothing doesn't exist. You can't hold on to nothing.

Air? Nope. Air isn't it either.

Come on, it's obvious. So obvious it's invisible. Give up? (I'll assume some of you never give up, and go ahead anyway).

You are holding on to an open hand. An open hand gives you the opportunity to choose. This is freedom. Now, pick something up with that same hand. Hold on to whatever it is. You are now holding on to a structure. This is security. Security may be any "Thing" that has a structure or pattern that you hold on to. This could be money, or any physical object, or even a relationship. We "hold on" to relationships by holding on to a role. The role of good husband may allow me to feel secure that I "have" a wife. The role of good worker may allow me to feel that I "have" a job.

What if we need to change the role? What if what we are holding on to doesn't make us feel secure? We usually let go of whatever it is. It seems structure can either be held on to or let go of. It's only the one, or the other. The moment that you held on to the structure (security), you simultaneously let go of your open hand (freedom). Now, if you *let go* of that object, or role, you will simultaneously be *holding on* to your "open hand." *Whenever you are holding on to freedom, you will be letting go of some security. Whenever you are holding on to security, you will be letting go of some freedom.* Or so it seems. On one hand.

On the other hand, most of us have another hand. We Have Another Hand! The other hand of space gives us time. Time isn't money, remember? Time is only worth something when you spend it. Time is not a "having-thing." Time, on the other hand, is a "being-thing." Even when we hold on to our security, our other hand may be held open to choose. Even if we hold on to the openness of freedom, our other hand can grasp what we need to feel secure. In time we learn to use both hands.

When we begin any new role, it's like a journey. Initially, we study the map with both eyes, and hold on to it with both hands. When we begin to move, we handle the map differently. Perhaps we need to keep one eye on it, one hand on it, and the other hand and eye on the road. When we are familiar with the route, we fold the map up and hold it in the glove compartment.

On one hand, you can remember. On the other, imagine.

Even if we can't tell the truth we can always be honest...

Truth or Lies *and...*

I never recommend lying. I don't always recommend the truth, either. I always encourage honesty, which can have very little to do with the Truth. The truth is a neutral force. Honesty values the empowerment of self and others.

Fortunately, the forefathers of the United States had foresight. They knew that the Law and Laws do not make Justice. Law provides an opportunity for justice, a possibility, a potential. And you and I both know that the law is not always just. People take advantage of opportunities. People take advantage of the law. Laws can serve many masters. Laws can be used for injustice. There are those times and places where any rules you follow just don't help. Where the "right" thing to do will injure you or someone else. Where action needs to be taken, and it doesn't quite follow the standard operating procedure, the status quo, moral climate and the Law.

I'm not going to describe the what's when's and where's here. I'd just be making up more "laws." But it happens. At times, honorable men and women feel they must break the laws of their land. Sometimes to retain their integrity and self-respect. Sometimes to maintain their very lives and the lives of those in their care. After they take these actions they may be brought to "justice." If they are on the witness stand, and they tell the *Truth* of their behavior, they will bring themselves to harm. If they are on the witness stand and they tell a *Lie* about their behavior, they will come to harm. Lying hurts us. Lying hurts us because it allows us to create an illusion of commitment and consistency. Security requires a solid foundation, a structure that can be built upon, just as our bones and teeth are firm enough to support the muscles, tissues and organs that keep us alive. When we lie, we put cracks in that foundation; we break the bones of our self image. One solution here is the *Fifth Amendment* of the U.S. constitution. "I refuse to answer on the grounds that it may tend to incriminate me." This allows us to still be honest.

The truth is that we can still be honest without telling the truth. The Truth is that sometimes I honestly don't want to tell you the truth of what I think, or see, or feel, or imagine. If I have not kept my personal word with you, if I have broken a commitment, well, then it is your business. Here I need to tell you. Otherwise my lie will stay between us like a wall. No matter how much you do to prove that you love me, or respect me. I can shut you out with the simple phrase:

"If you only knew… " For me, as long as I have kept my integrity or commitment, as long as all of my promises to you are kept, any other "truth" is my business. I'll share it only when it does some good and no harm. Sometimes, I just keep it to myself. Honestly.

If you haven't guessed it so far, this is the central theme of the book…

Guidelines to Freedom and Security

1. Freedom is the opportunity to be responsible for your own behavior. Another word for freedom is independence. We can "be" free. We cannot "have" freedom. Our thoughts and plans about independence in the future are concerns for the *security of our freedom*. In this sense, freedom always and only exists right here, right now.

2. Security is the opportunity to be responsible for another's behavior and/or to have another be responsible for us. Any commitment we make *to, for, or with* helps us to feel secure. Security is for this moment and the future. We can "have" security in the form of roles with others and in relation to ourselves. As a parent or child we have the security of a structured form of relationship. Another word for security is interdependence.

3. Human beings are never solely independent or interdependent, but both concurrently. We are simultaneously dependent on others and ourselves to survive and grow.

4. Many of our conflicts relate to the attempts to make security more important than freedom or freedom more important than security.

5. We cannot be free unless we have security; we cannot have security if we are not free. The homeless are free, and convicted

felons are secure behind bars. The debate over which has a "better" life is nonsense, as are most of our arguments attempting to make one state of being more important than the other. If we are trapped, we will value our escape. If we are without the shelter of belonging, we will value being imprisoned.

6. Saying that you need "space" is simply another way of saying you don't want to feel responsible for anyone but yourself. (As some of us are trained to feel continually accountable and obligated towards others, *out of sight* may be the only way to keep another *out of mind*). Sometimes we need to have this space, just as notes in music need a measure of silence between them. Otherwise there is just noise.

7. Saying you need to be "closer" is another way of saying you are insecure, and have a need you can't fulfill yourself. This has little to do with weakness, and much to do with gaining strength. All of us need the reflections of others to assure us of some aspect of our own existence. Your security will ultimately be up to *both* you and others.

8. If another has an investment in your insecurity, you will be insecure as long as you are dependent on them for what you desire. In this case, most of us learn to deny our needs, and/or blame ourselves for not being good enough to be acknowledged. This rarely changes anything, except to make us more deprived.

9. We need to realize that others are, at times, incapable of giving or receiving, and that we are not the cause nor are we the solution for their problems. The most caring thing that we can do here, (after first expressing our needs), is to let go and engage with others who can validate us.

10. Your security will ultimately be interdependent with others. Your freedom will depend on you. No one else can make you free.

QUESTIONS ON IDENTITY

1. Define the differences between freedom and security in terms of responsibility.

2. When and where and with whom do you feel the freest?

3. When and where and with whom do you feel the most secure?

4. How does the other help you in these areas?

5. What are the most important principles or values you live by?

6. Are there times you broke these or made exceptions?

7. What's the difference between true and false guilt?

Do You believe in UNCONDITIONAL LOVE?

**I Do. I WANT TO. Just don't ask me to define it.
The moment we define the unconditional we are
setting conditions. Caring for others does not exclude
care for the self. When it does we are being irresponsible martyrs. When caring for self excludes compassion for others we are being irresponsible tyrants.
Let's take a look at what care and love and intimacy
are all about...**

Chapter 5: Caring In Relationships

As fair and compassionate as we would like to be with others, often we find ourselves feeling burnt out, betrayed, and exploited. In some cases, we are completely innocent, and our partner was simply using us. We believed the lies and manipulations and were fooled. (*Anyone* can be fooled sometimes). However, in most instances of long-term neglect or abuse with an adult partner, we have participated in our own undoing.

We had a hidden agenda, concealed even from ourselves. It isn't that we wanted to be mistreated as much as we were terrified to be considered selfish, controlling and demanding – or gullible, bleeding-heart suckers.

These aspects of our identity will be given away (at great cost) to the other. Whatever we abhor, fear and declare, as "*Not Me*" will eventually link us to those who act out the behaviors we have disowned.

Love is an inclusive process. This means that love includes the giver and receiver. As adults, if we are to act in a loving way for our partner, this way must also be loving to ourselves. As parents with our children, we do need to sacrifice. There is a major difference between needing to care for someone and wanting to. There are also times when we do both together.

Here you will learn why the shirt off your back is not a gift that a true friend would accept. The covert deals of saints and sinners are explored, both inside and outside of us. There are guides here helping to identify caring that empowers and types of care that harm. You will discover why forgiveness can't be given for free, and how boundaries insure intimacy. You will learn how love and hate are connected. There are specific guides for sabotaging relationships and master-baiting your partner. Some notions of what love really can be are also presented in guideline form.

The general aspect of being a friend is accepting the other as your equal...

Some Friend

I always believed that I should give the shirt off my back to a friend in need. So I did until I was down to my last item of clothing. I started off with one friend without a shirt, and I ended up with one friend without a shirt – me. I don't really think that's what they mean by "progress." And, it occurred to me if that other person was my friend, that they wouldn't have taken my last shirt in the first place.

So now, I don't give the shirt off my back to friends.

But I still give it to those who are sick, wounded or to children – to anyone who can't really come through for themselves.

As long as they can't take care of themselves, I don't treat them as friends or equals. I treat them as I would the injured and children, those who need some direction. I may have to set rules and limits to help them heal and grow up. These rules can't belittle or diminish them. When you give in this manner, that doesn't mean that the other can or will reciprocate. When kindness given expects kindness back and receives nothing, sympathy turns into contempt. Both are ways of looking down at someone.

Just remember that pity and contempt are opposite sides of the same coin of small change. Go for the richer currency of respect and acceptance.

Why most of us think it's fair to be unfair...

The Jesus/Judas Trip

When I was a little kid I didn't know the word "relax." I didn't have to know it, 'cause I just did it. (The relaxing part, that is). Now that I'm a "grown-up," it's harder. Before, it was important to get out of school so that I could get a candy bar, watch television, play with someone, or ride my bike down that long hill in town. There was so much to see and do for the very first time.Later on it was flirting, romance and sex and true love. Still later it was being powerful, and respected, and important and successful. Now, it's just about being happy.

Back then I did the usual stuff, you know, proving that I was different from my parents by standing for everything they stood against. I went along with my friends to be popular, never guessing they were doing exactly the same thing with me. It makes me wonder what we all would have really done if we weren't busy proving how cool we all were. Me, I got into doing anything for most anybody just so they liked me. I always felt like I was some actor who played this part that people liked. They liked the role, though, not me. That's what I thought.

It was me who didn't like myself in the role. But, there were very few parts that I ever auditioned for. I was too afraid of not getting what I really wanted. Sort of like playing Jesus, martyring myself. It means that you give people whatever they want, despite the cost. I became a kind of chameleon that takes on the colors of its environment.

Hey, chameleons get along. With everybody but themselves.

When chameleons are alone, they have nothing to change into. They have no one to get approval from, to impress, or to perform for. So I read a lot, (it was easier to think other people's thoughts than my own) or watched TV, or found some way to distract myself. I learned even more ways to give other people what they wanted. When I really began to get fed up with myself for being the appointed savior of everyone, I'd play Judas.

I call it the Jesus-Judas trip. You know, you give and give and give, and then get sick and tired of all of those people taking advantage of your "goodness," then: "IT'S MY TURN, SUCKERS!" That's right. Then you take and take and take. Some do it with just one designated loved one. This one person is supposed to reward us for selling ourselves out to all the others we allow to exploit us. They were supposed to recognize all of my hard work and effort in meeting other people's needs, and reading my mind besides I was too afraid to ask for anything. I was very good at seducing folks to become involved with me. After a honeymoon period, I'd expect them to repair all the damage I was doing to myself – to fill me up. They couldn't. I didn't give them my time or show my true colors. I already gave my time to strangers willing to validate me as "important" (Hell, when Ghandi told his wife he was giving up sex, quitting his job and leaving her and the kids to save India she must have felt *real* special too).

If you don't pick one significant other or your family to do this trip on, chances are you will turn on everyone else you were supporting. Then eventually, everyone can be perceived as leeches, never really caring about you. Then, after you let them drain you, you can try to get even. You might forget that you invited them to screw you in the first place, because you liked the feeling. When you begin to screw them, and they scream "rape" – boy are you surprised! Well, if you didn't get the invitation, or if the date is long over, what do you expect? When the errors of our ways strike home, we repent and seek forgiveness for our betrayal as a Judas.

Guess what we do to try to make up for it? We resurrect the

Jesus in us and we give and give and give and give again. Guess what happens next? Right. You get rid of Jesus and become Judas again.

There is a way to get off this merry-go-round. It takes some effort. One realization you may have to grasp is that *your need to be secure and free is just as important as anyone else's.* This means that anyone else's needs here are just as important as yours. If we add being selfless and selfish together... we get to become fair to others *and* ourselves. When we don't, we wind up like the next couple you'll read about.

The deals we make to insure commitment are not always bargains...

Reflections on Saint and Sinnerhood

I believe that most people around us are mirrors. We see ourselves in them. When we look at them we are, in some way, looking at ourselves. Whether you see good or evil you are looking at your self. Usually it's those aspects of your being that you are most afraid to acknowledge. For good reason. To accept these ways of being would make you *like him.* Or *like her.* And you don't want to like him. Or her.

After all, most saints were martyrs. Most sinners were the ones that helped to kill them. They have a deal. Reflecting each other. One was afraid to be selfish; the other afraid to be selfless. So they set it up together to keep each other safe in the way they knew how to do best.

She set him up to be strong and rigid and logical, and pragmatic (she hated her father for being these things, and was not about to repeat his mistakes). He set her up to be weak and flexible, and dreamy, and frivolous (he hated his mother for being these things, and was not about to repeat her mistakes, either). They made a deal. She could be everything he was afraid of being, and he could be everything she was afraid of being. Now, they didn't make each other act in these ways, but each set the stage for the other's performance. Then, when the dance began they could hiss and boo. Their fights were not the punishment. The fights were the only way they could get some rest. The fights allowed them to retreat to neutral corners, spit out the blood, and come in fresh for another round. They had a deal. The real attacks came from the silences. Velvet gloved punches of silence that took their breath away. The jabs and hooks and uppercuts and combinations and roundhouses that voided real contact. They never learned to touch each other, except when it was time to hit below the belt. He finally got even by becoming a helplessly drunk. He became weak, and dreamy, and frivolous, anyway. She finally got even by becoming a strong, rigid, harping bitch that had good reason to be. Everybody said she had an excellent reason.

But they had a deal. So her strength stayed just weak enough so that she could continue to be a saint while being righteously angry. His weakness stayed just strong enough so he could continue to be a sinner while being righteously sad. They were right for each other; but not for themselves. They still couldn't see. They were not aware that it was all done with mirrors.

Blurry cold glass you can't see as your breath fogs it up. And after awhile, you have to turn toward something else. Because it's clouded over. Because you hate what you think you see. Because you don't want to be like him. Or her, (but you are). Sooner or later. So you might as well accept it before all the deals are made. Before all the contracts are signed. One thing may make it a little easier to bear. If all of us are indeed mirrors for each other, remember that most of the mirrors reflect imperfectly. Some are made in funhouses. They exaggerate and distort our features. What they show us may be a parody of ourselves. They may show what we look like first thing in the morning worst, or perhaps at our going out to town best. Remember that they usually only show us a portion of our Self, and that they almost never give us a clear view of the back of our head. Unless you remember that you are looking at yourself.

If we're going to judge behavior, let's do it in a way that empowers all who are willing to participate...

Guidelines for the Assessment of Behavior

1. Being able to name, label or identify anything is simply a way to bring order to an otherwise chaotic universe. Whenever we define another human being we are really defining how we are going to relate to that person. In this light, all definitions we make about others are really for and about ourselves.

2. All human behavior patterns can be artificially defined in a billion different ways. Our definitions can do more than just describe; they can also influence others to act in the ways we "expect" them to. At other times, our definitions will have little, if any, impact on the other's behavior, and their only practical use is in directing ourselves.

3. For the sake of brevity, there are five general ways to perceive all human behaviors. *Good, Bad, Sick, Dick-Like,* (Dick-Like could be seen as sexist, but it's really a synthesis of the Bad/Sick categories) and *Incapable*.

4. Good behavior empowers both the other and the self. It enhances capability and limits inadequacy. Good behavior is enacted without martyrdom, without "now you owe me," and without "after all I've done for you" guilt or shame. If there are any expectations of repayment, they are clearly defined and made prior to the interaction.

5. Hang out with people who consistently enact good behavior.

6. Bad behavior or "evil" is *intentional* exploitation or diminishing of the other in order to profit the self materially, emotionally, intellectually, or creatively.

7. Find a bigger stick than those who are enacting the bad behavior.

Show it to them and give them some very limited options. Be prepared to use it. If a bigger stick can't be found, get the hell away from them.

8. Sick behavior is the *unintentional* exploitation or diminishing of the other to profit the self in much the same way as "evil" behavior. The difference is the intent. There is no conscious desire to diminish or exploit at the others expense. However, the results are the same. In order for you to classify this pattern as "sick," the individual who is enacting the behavior must also:

a) Admit that this behavior is damaging to the other.

b) Commit to seeking and finding qualified help to change this behavior.

c) Commit to following the directions of that help, provided these directions do not conflict with the integrity of the self. When someone has lost all of their marbles and is more than a few sandwiches short of a picnic they may not be able to accomplish this stuff. If this is the case, wait until they've been released from the locked ward prior to any contact.

9. Since those that act with bad intent lie, if someone admits to sickness you better double check that they are keeping their commitments to get healthy.

10. You can hang out with people who are ill, but you may need to limit times for visiting hours. Be prepared for their sick behavior. You can be compassionate here as long as you avoid catching what they've got. The moment you start diminishing them or exploiting them you are in danger.

11. Dick-Like behavior is exactly the same as "sick" behavior. It exploits and diminishes without conscious intent. The difference is there is no admission or commitment to the necessity for change. If you beat them with a bigger stick, you get to feel guilty, and if you hang out with them, you get to be hurt. You can not help those with

dick-like conduct. You may delude yourself that being with them demonstrates true goodness and compassion. Actually, you are just being another "dick" to yourself.

12. Stay away from those exhibiting dick-like qualities as much as possible.

13. Individuals who are incapable are simply inept and incompetent. You don't have to heal them or punish them. Just don't let them drive your car and stay off the road when they are behind the wheel.

14. There is hope for all of us. It's just not always up to you to personally supply it.

Co-dependency or Care-taking appears compassionate for others while keeping everybody stuck in a bad game. Care-giving is a viable alternative...

Guidelines for Responsible Care-Giving

1. Caretaking is accomplished for the self. It usually diminishes all participants. Care-giving is accomplished for both the self and others. It empowers all that are involved.

2. Responsibility to another human being relates to one's capability to respond in a manner that can enhance the self, other, and relationship. Responsibility is often confused with obligation or duty. No one is obligated to accomplish something beyond his or her capability. If you or someone else puts you in this particular position, there is a hidden agenda to prove how incompetent you really are.

3. Whoever said, "It is more blessed to give than to receive" was more likely a receiver than a giver. It is blessed to be able to enjoy both forms of behavior.

4. If your care-giving takes more from you than what it allows you to receive, and you end up hurt and resentful, you are being a caretaker.

5. You can't invest in someone's welfare if they won't accept your support. (Though you can provide an opportunity for increasing their acceptance, provided that what you have to offer can translate into what they want to receive).

6. There is necessary pain, anger, fear and frustration that each of us must accept. Pain allows us to identify our injuries and to develop compassion. Anger allows us to accept our strengths and establish limits with others. Fear allows us to acknowledge threats and danger. Frustration can force us to accept our limitations as well as providing the drive to push beyond them.

7. Care-givers will support the other's right to all these feeling states without necessarily supporting the actions that may accompany them.

8. Care-givers offer the other an opportunity to contribute to the relationship. They may do so through exploring what particular resources the other does possess, and allowing the other to reciprocate. Caretakers usually ignore the other's attributes and belittle them by refusing to accept any contribution.

9. Care-takers identify themselves as selfless and nonjudgmental. They are selfish in holding on to an image of being unlike those selfish and judgmental bastards/bitches they have sacrificed all their lives for... Care-givers acknowledge that they are both are selfish and selfless. They are also judgmental. They realize that their judgments are merely opinions they do indeed have a right to. Most judgments of care-givers can be turned over in an appeal, provided there is sufficient evidence of change in the other's behavior.

10. Care-takers have a full time job, 24 hours a day, seven days a

week, with no time off for their good behavior. For caretakers, the reward for good behavior includes taking on more work. Care-givers take time off whenever possible, and structure their time to provide opportunities for play and relaxation. Care-takers take time off only when they have worked themselves to the point of illness and usually take vacations in hospitals.

11. These guidelines do not necessarily apply when dealing with infants, children, or anybody who happens to be passed out unconscious at your feet.

Even if they don't apply, these guides can be included in your considerations.

Our choices are only as constricted as our vision...

Freedom or Death

The abortion issue is a tough one for me. Here we can impose a law which will allow the unborn a chance to live. Here we will also impose a law that will allow choice itself to be disallowed.
Freedom or death.
If we choose for life, we also choose to restrict the choice of what a woman can do with her own body. Here we are saying that abortion is murder, and the taking of a life is a criminal act. So here we murder choice instead. Since most Pro-Lifers I know support the death penalty, I get perplexed here. If a human life is sacred, then how do we justify taking the lives of criminals and foreign enemies?
Then again, I get confused with those Pro-Choicers against the death penalty. They also terminate with or without extreme prejudice. If we are talking about the potential life any human has as being sacred, then we should outlaw both the death penalty and abortion. If, however, we are talking about the individual's right to choose what they can do to insure the quality of life for themselves, then we need

to allow the taking of life.

Either way we murder something. Now, if only those pro-lifers would be willing to adopt the children of the pro-choicers, wouldn't that be something? This goes for all you religious institutions out there too. Get together, set up adoption agencies, and set some financial structures to support the medical costs and economic losses of pregnancy. Raise these kids to be pro-lifers and take over.

The "take over" would depend on all those kids after eighteen years. Then you can fight with them about their values. In the meantime, put your money where your mouth is. If life is that sacred, it is worth any cost, isn't it?

As for you pro-choicers, well, to be against abortion is a choice, too. If choice is sacred, so is the other's right to choose differently from you. Support the right to make a choice. It's why the ACLU supports communists and fascists, black militants and the KKK. I don't really believe that civil laws ever have that much impact on morality. People have their ways of getting what they think they need or want.

As a man, I do not feel fit to judge or legislate what a woman should do with her body (Unless, of course, she asks for my opinion). My opinions are small, often not big enough to fit everyone at once. Most of my opinions are tailor-made. If there are any points of value I can make here, they will be small and simple ones. We need to make both life and choice equally sacred. Perhaps if we did, we wouldn't create the opportunity for what we call "necessary evil" to occur. For some of you, that evil may be the ending of a life. For others, that evil would be the ending of the right to choose.

So, I assume we'll continue to argue and debate without coming to any real solution. Mainly because there isn't one solution that we can or should impose for everyone. Freedom can never be forced. It can only be allowed. "Choices" that are imposed on you are simply chains in disguise. These shackles will have a weak link, and we will always look for a way to escape.

Unless, of course, you have forged the chains yourself. If you have, it might be a good idea to see if there are any other means that can keep you attached to what you value. If there aren't, then use your chains. I won't pull yours if you don't pull mine.

How do I love thee? Here are a few ways you can count on...

Love and Hate

I think that there are three basic ways to love someone:

a) Kiss Them: This includes all your warmth and gentle touches, thoughtfulness, and consideration. This is holding them when they cry, and being angry at those that have hurt them. This is the way we usually indulge those we care for.
This is *Love Making It Better For Now.*

b) Kick Them: This includes all the ways you may have to put your foot down with someone because they are screwing up their own integrity. It also includes all the ways you need to challenge them to exceed a limit they wish to overcome.
This is *Love Making It Better For Then.*

c) Leave Them: This includes leaving someone alone, or leaving the topic, or just plain leaving them. If they can't stop themselves, and kisses and kicks are ineffective, then what the hell else can you expect of yourself? This is *Love That Knows Better Than To Try And Make It Better.*

If you love someone, remember that at times you will also hate them. You may hate them for the power you have given them to effect you. You may hate them because they are the safest to hate. You may hate them because they love you, and you think there is something wrong with them for that. Well, maybe they see something in you that you can't see at the moment. (There is that remote possibility...)

Now, the same behaviors that I mentioned as loving can outwardly appear no different than the ones we use to hate. We can act with affection, if only to make another jealous, or to get even. A kiss can be used to betray. We can kick someone or leave because we are mean and inconsiderate. The foundation of love is built from intent. However, I'd like you to note that if you love anybody with just *one* of these ways it turns into something rotten.

Total indulgence sets people up to be selfish. Constant confrontation sets people up to be doubtful of their capabilities. Always leaving a problem still leaves the problem. So, love must be used in different ways at different times. But there can be an "always" in love. Love is the constant intention to make it good for both of us. That's what this love thing is all about – A beautiful song. If the notes have gone sour for you, the next selection may help

Familiarity may breed both contempt and security. Most of this is brought to us by a previous commercial sponsor who sold us a bill of goods...

Record Player

We play the songs together. You and me. Sometimes I am the Player. And you are the Record. No matter how I play with you, you only sing the old songs. You've sung them so many times even you must be bored. Your grooves have worn into ruts. The wheels get stuck. Ruts like deep canyons of shadow-hidden echo.

But I am only the player. And whatever I say, it probably feels as if I'm needling and scratching you. I know there are other songs to sing, hidden there. And they are in you, somewhere. They are the faint pastels, such delicate colors. They are also the reds of passion's dawn, the golden warmth of veiled light, the serenity of a blue ocean sky.

Instead of a needle, a soft brush would do. When you were touched, the colors would reveal themselves. When I am so busy painting my own pictures, I am blind to the songs. So, I will look with both ears, and listen with both eyes to uncover all shades light and dark. The canvass of music is often Silence.

Blame is the common ground men and women use to keep us distant from accountability...especially in relationships.

Nuts and Bolts

Nuts have these holes in them. Bolts have this intense desire to screw them. If the nut didn't have the hole in the first place, well, it would be very difficult to get screwed. Now, the nut could blame herself for having the hole. The truth is, she had very little to do with it. Somebody else put that emptiness there. She can't even see it. But she can sure as hell feel it. So she looks to be filled up. To stop the endless whispers that are shrill and seductive, reminding her of what was taken away. The echo of that injury sings with each breath of every empty word she hears. There are more than enough bolts available. She finds one. He screws her. She now has someone who makes all the echoes come alive. She now has someone to blame. He is such a BOLT.

Bolts have this sharp point, imagining that almost all nuts are offering open invitations. Bolts always assume that once a connection is made, the nut will hang on for dear life. Yet it is the bolt that has the threads that trap and hold. His threads are invisible to him, as is his single-mindedness. Bolts are so full of themselves they don't know what they are missing. Bolts often don't have a clue. Most feel obliged to thrust themselves into any new situation. Especially to keep them distant from their own desire for attachment. She is such a NUT.

Their need for completion connects the two of them to parts they would disown. She often refuses to make a point for herself. He avoids the emptiness that plagues him. They toss and turn, unable to make the connection, even though they're made for this joining. If they only knew... they could be building something beautiful.

Here are a few sordid games that I've watched clients play throughout the years.

Masters of Baiting

They were master baiters. Both hooked on it. It was their dance, their art, their sport, much like those folks who sit and make flies for fishing. I've seen them there with a pair of long needle-nose pliers attaching bits of fluff and otherwise useless bits of inconsequential garbage to a sharp hook. They throw the hook out at the end of a line that deceptively floats on a calm brook or stream. Waiting on the surface of things to engage a bite.

I wanted to say "Look out, you stupid fish, You're about to get hooked again!" (I did say that, but it didn't work). They were always more than ready to take the bait again. When I really looked close, it was hard to tell who was the fish and who was the fisher. Both always had a way of angling themselves into it. Both knew what the other "really" thought, and "really" wanted to say. They cast the lines out with precision and grace. The lines always tangled and snagged.

To catch something, you need to know about traps and your prey. First you need the lure. This is your bait. You need to know the appetite of what you're after. Besides the lure you need the hook that the other gets caught on, or the bars that snap into place, or the noose that tightened. Now if the bait and trap are one and the same, you've got poison. Advanced master baiters often use this as their final resort.

It hadn't reached that stage with them. They mainly worked with the right/wrong-barbed hook. In order to make this hook really work, both have to have an investment in being Right or Wrong. If you have an investment in being wrong, you make bait out of your passivity, or forgetfulness. You keep reminding the other of this with continual apologizing. Be supplicating – If you have the investment of being right, you make the bait out of your activity and recall of detail. You keep reminding the other by ignoring their strengths. Be righteous. The game of master baiting is designed with only one goal in mind.

To keep you stuck. You can master-bait by yourself, but it's a game that's open to couple and group participation (although modern science has scoffed at the evidence, master baiting stimulates the growth of palm hair and other werewolf attributes). It can also create severe depression and explosions, especially when played by couples.

We need one player who is afraid of being aggressive. Their goal will be to maintain their submissiveness while getting the other to beat on them. Until…they are then justified in acting out with violence, or until they have fulfilled their need to be punished for some past shame or guilt. The other player will be afraid to be vulnerable or submissive. They must keep their position of authority and provide the lures that will create the opportunity for the first player to feel inadequate and incompetent. They can do this until the "weak" one lashes out. Then, and only then will the "strong" one let themselves become open and vulnerable. Of course the player they have just infuriated will now react with aggression. Even if they now respond with apologetic care, something can be found "not good enough" about the execution of such nurturing. The authority has always experienced humiliation, pain, and guilt in being needy. They continue to have to be right about this. Then we go back to the opening lines of the player who is in the submissive position.

The game resumes. There are no apparent winners to the outside observer. If you look closely, you'll see how each is really helping the other. The submissive player may be terrified of initiating any authority. The dominant player may be terrified of initiating any vulnerability. Each protects the other from having to accept these moves as necessary and useful ways of being. When the subordinate gets strong, it either pushes away or "hurts" the other. When the authority gets weak, the submissive other is so peeved by this time that take the opportunity for revenge. Both are reassured that what they are afraid of being has good cause.

Both are protected. It's the protection that you give someone when you let them keep using crutches when their legs are healed. Or, like the type of care you get when someone encourages you to exercise legs that are still broken. In both cases the care isn't really care giving. It takes away something from what the other needs to do or be. However, if the players keep at it, they can both win by becoming so disgusted enough with each other they split up for good. This is the simplest form of the game.

I know I could go on and describe the moves and counter moves for the higher ranked players. However, the game is a really boring one unless you are actively playing. When you are a player, well, it's Life and Death. There are a few good ways to screw up Master-baiting for couples. I usually don't try to talk anyone out of playing, unless the game has reached that poisonous stage of physical violence. If it does, then I add the rule that "one more time" of assault will end my relationship with that couple. In my opinion, they need to separate and work out how they've become what they are. If they refuse to do this, I won't play referee. Also, I let them know that if I am designated ref for the game, any information they give me must also be presented to their opposing player.

This means revealing affairs, addictions and other actions that can jeopardize the welfare of their partner. Otherwise I end up hooked myself. The lures that are thrown out are fun for me to mess with. You see, master baiting has to have the proper bait to catch what you're looking for. If you are caught up in being submissive, the bait will be stuff designed to help you feel "wrong," weak, helpless, or not good enough. If you are caught up in being an authority, the bait will be stuff designed to help you feel "right," strong, helpful, or competent. So, whenever either party throws that bait out, I attach some other bits of fluff to it that reverse it's appearance. I show how the weak take care of the strong, which is helpful.

-How those who are wrong make the other right, which is right to do.

-How those that must be strong are helpless in having to control.

-How the authority is always dependent on dependency.

And so on. Any way you play this game, if one person wins, the other looses. If your partner looses, then you loose too. The only way for both parties to win is if they become tied into accepting each other as equal partners. This means that both get to make the rules for a different game.

God, I hope so. Imagine being trapped, 24 hours a day, watching those fishing shows on cable for the rest of your life.

More on the need for boundaries. If we cannot be separate, we cannot join...

Guidelines for Boundaries

1. Boundaries are walls we make to house our rights of self-direction. A wall protects us with security and allows us freedom within its limits. Besides this, it protects our neighbors from being annoyed by whatever loud noises we may care to make.

2. Most of us get easily offended through being excluded by another's limits. Yet, all homes have walls that accomplish this same purpose. Walls also protect us from the outside elements, insure our privacy, and help us complete a variety of useful tasks without distraction.

3. Expecting people to knock down their walls for us and expecting ourselves to knock down walls for them can really screw up the home we all live in.

4. In human relationships, boundaries are verbal and nonverbal communications that serve as fences to limit the types of behaviors we will engage in. Breaking these boundaries can result in legal sanctions. Sexual abuse, child neglect, theft, assault, and any behavior that violates the rights of another human being are examples of this. Boundaries can also be the declarations we make about the amount of time and effort we will put forth in those activities that we do share together. Breaking these boundaries can result in civil and moral sanctions, and a whole lot of bad feelings besides.

5. In parent/child relationships, boundaries need to be set by the parents based on what the parent decides as good for the child's welfare without endangering the welfare of other children, the couple themselves, or the welfare of each parent as a functioning adult. Parents may need to sacrifice time, effort, money and egos. They are not to sacrifice their integrity or self respect.

6. In adult relationships, boundaries need to be *mutually* set for the welfare of each individual and the relationship as a whole. The needs of each must be made equally important.

7. Boundaries, like walls, have an outside/inside. A boundary always allows you to say "No" to some behavior or activity while simultaneously allowing you to say "Yes" to something else. Walls without this depth often collapse due to their flimsy structure.

8. Doors make excellent boundaries. Here, we have a "No/Yes" that hinges on the changing needs of the self and the environment. Our hinges must not be attached to our emotions alone, but also to the rational use of authority and integrity as determinants of our actions.

9. The security of any relationship is only as strong as the degree of commitment all participants have in keeping their word.

There are times when escape is not so much avoidance but a necessity...

Bailing Out

If you are out on the water sailing, and for whatever reason you start to sink, well, – you need to start bailing. If it's a slow leak, you can even ignore it if you change your course and move toward a safe harbor.

The complete repair can take place there. If the leak is moderate, you need to stop what you have been doing, find a container for what is sinking you, bail that stuff out and patch it up. You'll still need to get to the nearest safe harbor in this case too. However, if the integrity of the hull has been breached severely, you may sink regardless of how quickly you bail. In this case, we don't bail the vessel. We bail ourselves out of the vessel.

I believe that there is only one reason for a captain to go down with the ship. That's if there is one chance in hell to make a safe landing. Otherwise, if we're in a an elevated position, we have a responsibility to protect those in our charge who depend on us. (Airline pilots and parents take note). Those of us at sea level with each other don't have to worry about this.

The hard part to remember here is that some vessels can only be salvaged after they have sunk. Bailing out for now may be the only way to save yourself and those in your care.

Most of us would rather be proven right than wrong. Many of us have come to believe that we will never be able to depend on another human being for love and security. These guidelines are especially for you. In order to maintain our unalienable rights to be miserable yet correct, we must find ways to prove that others are neither willing nor capable of caring for us. The following guidelines will insure complete success in this effort. You can maintain your pain with dignity.

Guidelines for Sabotaging Relationships

1. Never directly inform the other of your needs. Later, as your needs are ignored by them, blame them for being selfish and inconsiderate.

2. If you do inform them of what you desire, make sure that you are as ambiguous as possible. This provides them even more opportunity to misread you and screw up.

3. If you are asking someone to take care of you, especially when you are vulnerable and needy, make sure that you demand such attention in a hostile manner. If anger is difficult for you, casually mention your requests in an off hand, nonchalant way, as if it makes no difference one-way or the other. In either case, act enraged or hurt when they don't come through.

4. An equally sabotaging move is to wait until the other is sick, in crisis, or extremely busy with some important task. Even when they do come through for you, you can then complain about how their bad attitude ruined their efforts.

5. If you are demanding that the other respect you and pay attention, remember to whine and act pathetic. Promise them that you'll do anything, anything at all if they'll only respect you. This always guarantees further disrespect, (at the very least you'll disrespect yourself), which you can blame them for later. So simple, and it really, really works!

6. The moment when the other has finally come around and actually demonstrates love and care, bring up some past negative incident, accuse them of some betrayal, or find something else to complain about.

7. Refuse to participate in any activities that the other enjoys. Better yet, go on these outings and become sullen and moody. If you have an audience, create a scene.

8. Respond to any spontaneous show of love and respect with "You don't really mean that," or "What the hell do you really want?" Questioning the other's motives is an ideal way to deflect actual care.

9. Instead of informing your spouse or significant other about your feelings of neglect or abuse, tell a best friend or close relative. Make

sure the one you tell will be on your side, right or wrong. Then, make up with whomever you had been in conflict with and fail to inform your original confidant. (Who can begin to despise your partner). Later on you can complain how the relationship has alienated you from friends and family.

10. If you are in a monogamous commitment, have an affair and don't tell the other on the pretext, "It would only hurt him or her." (And of course, "It didn't mean anything.") When your lover acts in a loving way towards you after this, your guilt can act as an excellent wall to shut out any positive support. Remember that they don't love the *"real you,"* – just the *you* they think you are...

11. Forget birthdays and anniversaries. If you do remember, make no special plans, and buy no presents. If you have made plans, and have bought presents, find a way to charge them to the other's checking or credit.

12. Continue to bring up old flames, or stare attentively at attractive strangers in the other's presence. Deny it when you are caught red handed.

13. If you are enjoying playing, relaxing, or making love, begin to dictate new rules that the other has never agreed to follow.

14. Give your significant other complete responsibility for your happiness and welfare. (Or take on complete responsibility for theirs). If anything goes wrong in your life, blame the other for it and make them feel obligated to fix it for you. (Or completely blame yourself for not being able to change their situation). Continue to stress the hopelessness of the relationship in bursts of anger or sobbing and/or become mute and distant. When the other begins to express their own insecurity about themselves, inform them that you have more important things to attend to than to listen to their pathetic whimpering.

15. If your significant other has behaved in any way mentioned in these sabotage guidelines, show them exactly where they are screwing up and rub their nose in it. Better yet, humiliate them with this information in public with close friends and family. It's fun for everyone! (Well, almost everyone, but you knew they weren't really going to keep loving you anyway, right?)

Whether you're in love or it doesn't mean a thing...doesn't really make a difference here

Affairs to Remember

Sexual infidelity is about breaking commitments. It's about lying and cheating in the name of love or fun or that "moment of weakness" or whatever other stupid excuse we happen to make up at the time. If you are the "other" in the affair and you really love that man or woman you are cheating with...think this through. True love means you are acting to empower that individual, that you value their happiness and welfare. Part of anyone's welfare is his or her principles. Participating in an affair sets up your lover to damage his or her own integrity. Having an affair enables the cheater to stay in what may be a cruddy relationship anyway. If he or she has no morals don't fool yourself into thinking you're so special that they will be faithful to you. They've already broken that promise to someone else, and any promises about leaving are usually just as bogus. One thing you have to consider here is that you may not really want an available and committed relationship. Pick on someone who's single to avoid hurting the other innocents involved.

If you are the "adulterer," why are you staying with your original partner? If you use your children as an excuse, be advised that you're teaching them to become hypocrites, as you're busy faking it. Is this what you want them to learn? If you *"love"* your partner or spouse then doesn't that person deserve the opportunity to be with someone who really is *"in love"* with them? As long as you are with them, you deny them that chance for real happiness.

If it "really doesn't mean anything," remember that lies serve to make walls that block our reception of love, – even when we are truly loved. Does he or she love the person you are or just who they think you are?

This question will never be answered as long as you are dishonest.

In my experience, the guilty party here becomes incapable of really feeling loved by the faithful partner and behaves in ways to sabotage closeness and provoke hostility. Both partners are miserable and the circle of strife continues...You may have to explore here your need to punish all who are involved.

If you are that "other man or woman," end the affair until the other reveals their involvement with you and terminates their previous commitment. If you are the "cheater," then do the very best you can to make things work out with your committed partner. These include ending the affair, seeing a therapist and even confessing to your indiscretions. If you're unwilling to work these things through, then stop being so selfish and get the hell out. If you have an "arrangement" with someone that it's okay to have an open sexual relationship, good luck. I've never seen them work for long. For the rest of you who think you can eat your cake and have it too...Maybe you can if you don't mind the taste of puke. I recommend swallowing pride and seeking forgiveness...

Forgiveness is a process requiring participation from the guilty as well as the innocent. Most of us fool ourselves into thinking we can forgive all by ourselves...think again.

Forgiveness

This is for you who have been hurt by somebody.

I guess this means all of us. There are two ways that another person hurts us. The first way is by their actions. We could be physically abused, as in being beaten, or raped. We could be emotionally abused, as in being verbally degraded or humiliated. Abuse can come from anyone, whether they are family, friends, acquaintances, or strangers.

The second way of getting hurt is by neglect. Neglect is an act of omission. If a person has hurt you in this manner, it is because they didn't fulfill an obligation to take care of you in some way that they agreed to.

Now, "why" someone has abused you or neglected you always depends. It always depends on who is asking. The doctor may blame biochemical reactions. The psychotherapist may blame a traumatic childhood. The defense will blame the victim. The prosecution will blame the perpetrator. I would suggest that you, whoever you are, realize that asking yourself "why" will not accomplish anything. (Except perhaps, avoidance of what you may need to do). If you are reading this, you are not a victim. You are a survivor.

The difference between the two is a simple one. Survivors are alive, and victims are dead. To further the process of healing and recovery, there are certain actions any survivor needs to take. The ultimate recovery is to forgive. However, *there are conditions that are prerequisites to forgiveness.* If someone has harmed you, they have to do some work. So do you. To err is human, to forgive, divine. So let us remember that we are human, and only want-to-be's in the divine department.

A) If someone does not admit to his or her abuse or neglect of you, then supposedly not even God forgives. If you "forgive" someone who won't even confess they have harmed you, you are being more than divine. You are being arrogant. The perpetrator must acknowledge the abuse or neglect to you.

B) If someone admits to an action, but refuses to commit to a new type of behavior toward you, then forgiveness means that you have just okayed a repeat performance. Here you have jeopardized yourself and the other, especially if the other does not have the capability to control their own behavior.

C) Finally, there must be consequences, or atonement or amends that are mutually agreed upon by the parties involved. This must be carried through. If they aren't, you can assume that the offender will feel enough guilt to set you up to punish them. If you do, there is the danger that you will become...

Just Like Them. A Perpetrator.

If you are a survivor, your job is to confront the perpetrator, or abuser, or negligent with their actions. You need to ensure your own safety in this process to the best of your ability. This means that you don't keep whatever it is a secret, nor do you use it to blackmail, extort, control, or diminish the other. Use a friend, shrink, man of the cloth, cop, attorney, relative, etc.. If these conditions for forgiveness are not met, and if there is no way to ensure your safety in taking these actions, Do not forgive.

Get your ass out of there, instead. Some people are like animals, blinded by their pain and hunger. Their abuse or neglect is not intentional. You still need to protect yourself. Walls of time and distance may be necessary until the other's pain is healed, or their hunger satisfied. People may be incapable of admitting to their incapability's here. If this is the case, you can forgive, but your walls may have to remain intact. Some creatures enjoy killing and maiming. They take a malicious pleasure in the suffering of others, and inflict that suffering whenever they can get away with it. They will then lie to your face in order to get the opportunity to take advantage of you again. Don't let them. Here there is nobody to forgive, because there is no one home. We do not forgive cancer. We remove it, or contain it so it doesn't spread. Remember that you are a survivor. As you take these necessary actions you get to survive. And one thing more. Your fate is returned to your own hands. You get to be alive again, in all the ways you need to live.

You even get to love.

These are guides, not ultimatums or absolutes. Use them accordingly.

Guidelines to Love

1. Love is the sum total of feelings, thoughts, and actions directed towards enhancing both security and freedom of self and other. We often confuse passion with love. Desire is only the surface. The depths of love are filled with our consideration, our commitment – and especially our actions.

2. Loving another requires us to value other's needs and welfare as much as we value our own. Consequently, we cannot love another if we act unloving to ourselves. Love requires the acceptance of both self and other, denying neither.

3. Love requires more than words to be understood, more than affection to be felt, and gifts to be appreciated. Loving requires words that touch, feelings that understand, the presence of time freely shared and actions that cherish.

4. Loving is like the ocean, a constant force that circles the island of our solitude. Being *in love* is passion's flow of waves. They may seem to retreat and can always return if we preserve the ocean from which they come. To do so, we must maintain our friendship, trust and respect.

5. Love is one part compulsion and one part choice, together transforming obligation into preference.

6. For some, saying "I love you" is the most difficult act of all, while their loving behavior is an everyday constant that may be taken for granted. For others, performing loving acts is a rare occasion, yet their verbal declarations of caring appear interminable. Talk is cheap when there is a vast quantity of it. Actions speak louder than words

only when we listen with more than our ears.

7. "If you really loved me, you would..." not use this stupid phrase to try to guilt me into whatever it is that you want.

8. Love has a life of it's own, and like all life, must be nurtured to flourish. Love can become sick and die for lack of care. Unconditional love is an ideal illusion. Would you still love me if I shot you in the head? Perhaps the "soul" of your love may endure, but the embodiment of it can surely perish

9. Any love you truly give for free will only enrich you. However, like any rich nourishment, the milk of loving-kindness may cause weight gain, indigestion, and lactose intolerance. In these instances you may need to either change your recipe or go where your cooking can be really appreciated.

10. The only thing that you can really expect love to effect is your own sense of well-being. One gift that you can give yourself for being loving is the permission to walk away from those who are not.

11. You must always be included as an object of your own affection and compassion.

Here's another way to look at what "causes" problems and how to fix them...if you can remember that nobody's broken in the first place.

On Relationships:

A Self Analysis
There are more than a few reasons why many of us stay in screwed up relationships. Understanding "why" may be helpful. What's more useful may be to learn how our problem may also be a

solution.

As I've said before, all shit is fertilizer. (Unless you're tracking it on the living room floor. Then it's just smelly stuff you got to clean up). Besides, just might be that the relationship is not as messed up as you think. Exceptions here are when you wind up with partners that beat you, continually cheat on you, and are practicing addicts or alcoholics. Even if this is the case, get it out of your head that you "attract" people like this. This implies you have some mysterious power to draw others into your own little world of victim hood.

It's more likely that *you* are attracted to them. You may pick partners who may tend to be:

-Distant and emotionally unavailable. (Yet, at times, very passionate).

-Controlling, aggressive and judgmental.(Yet, at times, solid rocks to lean on).

-Helpless, weak and continually needy. (Yet, at times, affectionate and tender).

-Sometimes, any and all combinations of the above...

"Why" you are attracted to certain personality patterns has a great deal to due with your parents. Now, don't get into blame here. Your folks probably did the best they knew how to do. If they didn't, and deliberately abused you for fun and profit, then to hell with them. We need to honor our parents only if they are willing to act like parents. Otherwise what are we repeating? Maybe this is why Moses really threw the Ten Commandments down and busted them up. Our laws can't be written in unyielding and inflexible stone. There are exceptions to every rule, and rules we need to make about these exceptions. However, deliberately harming your kids is more the exception than the rule. If you were unintentionally neglected or abused you have the right to feel hurt or angry. You have the right to both defend and express yourself. You just don't have the right to be abusive. Nobody does.

Basically, we're all Bozos on the bus, taking our turns behind the wheel of parenthood or other positions of authority while learning to drive. Count on the fact that everybody can make mistakes. Even me and you.

The difficulty is, no one can really correct a mistake they won't admit. Keep that in mind as we go on...

SOME REASONS WE PICK RELATIONSHIP PARTNERS LIKE OUR PARENTS :

1) We're trying to resolve the same conflicts that we had/still have with mom and dad, or whomever had charge of us. (Even though some of our folks have mellowed with age, if we're not able to express our feelings of neglect or abuse in a constructive way, we'll tend to keep replaying the scenes).

2) We're deathly afraid of behaving like our parents in the ways which they hurt us the most. So, we set up our partner for that role which we must dread being ourselves. We may perceive being vulnerable as being weak, being assertive as being mean, being emotional as being out of control, being unemotional as being uncaring and so on. If we can never be assertive, because it's "mean," our partner is set up to make decisions and take control. If we can never be vulnerable and trust the other to take charge, our controlling sets them up to be passive and weak. And, at times we need to disengage from others, if merely because they and we have to be responsible for ourselves. It's not that we actually want to act or be treated this way. When we act in the same ways our caretakers acted, it brings up guilt and anxiety. For most of us, acting the opposite is a solution. Or so we'd like to think. It's also the problem.

3) To resolve these conflicts would mean creating fundamental changes in how we deal with our feelings, our beliefs and our own thinking. Quite frankly, this scares the shit out of us. (We fail to realize here that most of us are full of some shit or another, and it might be good to dispose of some, so let's deal with this area first...)

DEALING WITH FEELINGS
-OR BEING REALLY CHICKEN IS WHEN YOU WON'T COP TO IT

Now, most all of your feelings have value, like it or not. Expressions of vulnerability such as pain, fear, depression and anxiety allow us to communicate need, process loss and allow another to take charge. Your partner also gets to feel important and needed. Expressions of authority, such as anger, confidence, pride and assertiveness allow us to defend others and ourselves. Your partner may get a chance to feel protected.

Our passions can motivate us, just as our detachment allows us to rein ourselves in. When we go overboard with any one feeling, there's a good chance that we're using it to avoid feeling something else. If we are constantly angry, we may be using it to avoid our pain.

This may influence our partner to feel pain, in that they are set up to be helpless and not good enough. Constant sadness may be a way to avoid our anger. This may set our partner up to continually be trapped with the burden of authority we refuse to take on ourselves. In any case, we always need to check into our feelings as opposed to checking out.

Some questions for you here:

What feelings are you most afraid to express to your partner?

When your partner express's himself or herself, what feelings most upset you?

What do you do when you feel? What does your partner do?
Hurt?
Angry?
Afraid?
Ashamed?
Guilty?
Happy?
Passionate?
Tender?
Distant?

What feelings did you see your mother and father express to each other most often?

What could each express to you?

What could you express to them?

What couldn't you express?

What can't and won't you express now?

When's the last time you tried?

DEALING WITH BELIEFS AND ATTITUDES
-OR IF YOU BELIEVE LOVE CONQUERS ALL IT'S TIME TO GROW UP.

If you're good, good things don't always happen.

The only certain thing I know is that when I'm good, I get self-respect.

Getting anything else can be a crapshoot.

You can express yourself and not get the results you really want. It doesn't mean that you weren't good enough. It doesn't mean that you could have done anything differently. Sometimes your partner and others will not be able to see your caring or strength, nor your needs or pain. Sometimes they won't hear your compassion or concerns.

Sometimes they won't feel your same passion or tenderness.

Sometimes no matter how delicious the meal, somebody has the stomach flu. Sometimes they'll even blame it on your cooking.

All of us idealize certain behaviors. Which is why we also devalue them. Love, honesty, loyalty, knowledge, even logic… you know which one it is for you. You know – love conquers all.

(Let me clue you in. – Love doesn't want to conquer anything).

Somehow, we believe that when we manifest these traits that God or some other invincible force is on our side.

(Unfortunately, the Universe doesn't take sides in the way we think).

Just because you're acting based on your ideals doesn't mean you are going to win. Neither mercy nor righteousness provides any guarantees.

The first reason we make ideals omnipotent (all-powerful) is because we are afraid to admit that we're helpless about changing anyone.

It really is up to them, not us. We can't "make" people love us. We can only *allow* them to love us. (By the way, we also don't "find" ourselves. We really need to make ourselves into the person we wish to become. That's why you picked whom you picked... to help you).

The second reason we make ideals all-powerful is most of us feel giving up on someone is negligent and cold, – that we are abandoning them. This is not the case. You need to abandon the belief that you are the one that that will make the difference when you've done the best you can and it really hasn't made that difference. Valuing ideals as invincible creates a false sense of security that generates it's own collapse. If we make love everything, and give everything, then love means nothing and we have nothing left.

Most of us can't live with this, so instead we blame ourselves on not being good enough and keep an illusion of hope at the cost of our own esteem.

Love is not invincible or omnipotent. It's just the most important thing we can give and take.

Put that in your pipe and smoke it, keep it under your hat and save it for sunny and rainy days. And remember...the best you can is always good enough. Some questions for you here:

What were the values that were important in your family?

Father's?

Mother's?

Other family, friends and teachers you learned from?

Did your folks walk as they talked?

What do you value most about your character?

What do you value most about your partner's character?

Were you allowed to ask for support and validation?

What kind did you get?

Were you given the trust to do things on your own?

PARTNER PROJECTIONS AND YOUR PARENT'S NEGATIVE BEHAVIORS
OR – WHAT YOU MAY HAVE ASKED FOR ... AND HOW

Okay, – maybe you're tired of questions.

The real deal is, you have all the answers already inside. It just takes the right questions to bring them out. What I'd like you to do next is a little experiment.

LIST SEVEN BEHAVIORS OF YOUR PARTNER/FRIENDS/ ETC. THAT DRIVE YOU CRAZY.

These can things they do or things they don't do, including what they say or don't say. Be sure to include how you are effected negatively by this

1.
2.
3.

4.
5.
6.
7.

Take a look at these and make up five character traits that you think would describe such a person, based on their behavior.

1.
2.
3.
4.
5.

LIST TEN BEHAVIORS OF YOUR PARENTS THAT WERE HURTFUL AND/OR NEGLECTFUL.

You could use five from each parent, or whatever seems most appropriate.

1.
2.
3.
4.
5.
6.
7.
8.
9.
10.

Take a look at these and make up five character traits that you think would describe such a person, based on these behaviors.

Father	Mother
1.	1.
2.	2.

3.   3.
4.   4.
5.   5.

Now, list which of these traits your partner has in common with your parents.
   1.
   2.
   3.
   4.
   5.
   6.
   7.

If you haven't come up with any crossover traits, good for you.

Your problems in your relationship may be situational. Births, deaths, moving, job losses and anything else that creates stress will effect you as a couple. Another possibility is that one (or even both) of you may have a medical condition that effects your emotions and/ or thinking.

Otherwise, go on to…

TIME FOR A LITTLE ANALYSIS…
OR ANOTHER WAY TO SEE THIS STUFF
If, there are similarities, we need to explore them. One way is to start thinking about things in a different way. Here's how.

We can divide most human behaviors into three categories:

(Hey, we could divide them into a billion different categories, but three will do for now).

1) Submissive behaviors are communications we use to represent our limitations. Sadness, fear, doubt and inadequacy are some examples.

2) Dominant behaviors are communications we use to represent our capabilities. Anger, perseverance, certainty and competency are

examples here.

3) Symmetrical behaviors are communications that represent both categories at once, when we're both in control and out of control. Humor, playfulness and sexuality are all instances of this human expression.

Now I want you to think of the word "dependent." What comes to mind? Stuff like needy, weak, helpless, and confused? Probably. These are forms of submissive behavior. The opposite of submissive behavior is dominant behavior.

Think of the opposite of weak. Strong comes to mind. The opposite of needy is "giving, " while the opposite of helpless is helpful, and the opposite of doubt is certainty. So if dominant behaviors are the antithesis of submissive behavior,

- being strong, giving, helpful and certain must mean you are independent, right? Not quite. Because you see, in order to express dominance, the authority *needs* a subordinate. A *parent* can't be a parent without a *child.*

A *teacher* can't be a teacher without a *student.*

Each role is necessary for the other to exist. The truth is that considering yourself giving, helpful, competent and so on does not make you independent. An authority is *responsible for*; a subordinate is *responsible to.*

Both are dependent on the other for the role they play. Conversely, you can't really behave like a child if you have no parents. Not for long, at any rate.

We will reject *initiating* any and all of these necessary behaviors depending on how we were raised. We may make it **WRONG** to be an authority if we had an over controlling judgmental parent. We may make it **WRONG** to be a subordinate if we had an under controlling or absent parent. We will consciously reject accepting and manifesting the behaviors of whichever parent we felt most abused or neglected by. (Even though we may end up acting just like them when we feel cornered.

But it was us who painted the floor and got ourselves stuck there).

We may end up rejecting both aspects, maintaining a constant neutrality, distance and making a joke out of everything. Most of the time the jokes on us.

True independence can only be acquired by accepting **both** our limitations and capabilities. This sum of this being is not more than or less than. It's an integration that makes us complete. If we add the child and the parent together we get an adult. An adult expresses symmetrical behavior, the communication of an equal to another equal. It is not better or worse than the complementarity of dominance/submissiveness. It is different.

A symmetrical perspective values all roles equally, and can shift into the role that will be most empowering to self/other, *whatever* it may be. **STRENGTH** is flexibility, which again is a melding of all parts.

There are both negative and positive descriptions of the same behaviors:

Positive Value	Negative Value
Taking care of one's self	selfish
selfless	martyr-victim
self confident, assured	arrogant, cocky
thrifty	cheap
open, trusting	naive, gullible
vulnerable, receptive	weak, passive
strong	dominating, controlling
adaptive	placating
sensual	seductive
neutral	uncaring, cold
tenacious	stubborn
cautious	fearful
witty	sarcastic

and so forth…

Most of the problems that I see in couples come from the lack of integration and the rejection of some part of the self. This discarded part is usually given to the other to play. They usually volunteer and give us the parts they won't own. Then each can see the other behaving just like the parent with whom they had difficulty. ('Cause we swore we would *never* act like that).

We usually see the other we're with being just as bad, just as wrong as good old mom and dad and we get to avoid conflict with our folks and play pin the tail on the jackass we're with.

(We've had the tale for a long time and fortunately they are readily available). We get to avoid conflict with ourselves. We can keep disowning what and who we also need to accept in ourselves.

GETTING THE BALL ROLLING

Take a look at the so-called negative character traits of your parents and partners. Break them down into the three categories of dominant, submissive and symmetrical behaviors.

Then write about situations where and when these traits could be a positive force and eventually helpful for all those involved.

This may be a stretch for you. That's okay.

It's how we get the kinks out.

1. DOMINANT BEHAVIORS-

Taking control, making judgement calls, taking charge, being willing to confront, being unbending, assertion and anger, being actively non-receptive, denying pain and fear.

Think of the roles of parent, teacher, judge, boss...

Where and when is being an authority useful to you and others?

2. SUBMISSIVE BEHAVIORS

– Giving control and deferring to another, being open and receptive, refusing to confront, acknowledging pain and fear.

Think of the roles of child, student, employee...

Where and when is being a subordinate useful to you and others?

3. SYMMETRICAL BEHAVIORS

– Not really caring about control, being playful and humorous, (re-creational), valuing others behaviors as *different* vs. right or wrong.

Think of being a friend, a peer, a colleague an equal to another…

When and where is it useful to you and others?

We can transform the negative into the positive…if we respond instead of react.

Substituting Affirmation for Negation: A Basic Primer

All of us get frustrated at times with the behavior of others. People can be negligent, thoughtless, inconsiderate, cranky, insulting and just plain abusive.

This includes family, friends, co-workers and even strangers we meet by chance.

This is not always intentional on other people's parts. Some of them had bad days, some of us are space cadets and others are just plain miserable most of the time.

-The fact is, – we don't have control over other folk's behavior.

We only have control over our own.

Some of us think that we attract other people to our lives. This is rather narcissistic. After all, we could say that they attracted you to their life. Not that I'm saying there isn't some grand cosmic plan. Perhaps there is. I have enough trouble with this plane of reality.

You need to know that some people actually have an unconscious investment in our emotional reaction to them. They may be insecure, angry, or afraid and unwilling to accept or even admit this to themselves. So, they end up doing something called *projection*, – which is setting YOU up to feel what they are afraid to feel themselves. As I said this is usually not intentional, it's just one of the ways we humans use to cope with ourselves.

We *ALL* project at times, because all of us have hidden fears.

We may be afraid of being weak, or helpless or needy, or of being confused and uncertain. We may be afraid of being aggressive, or controlling, or of making the wrong decision. We may be afraid of being selfish, or of being used and exploited.

– Hell, we can be afraid of being ANYTHING.

Our fear is what screws up our own process of communication here, because we REACT instead of RESPOND.

Now, what I'm going to go over with you to help change this doesn't guarantee that you will always get your needs met, or that you'll "win" with everybody.

– Like I said, some folks do have an investment in screwing us over, intentionally or not, and sometimes the only thing we can do is get the hell away from them.

Otherwise, it helps to communicate our needs in an affirmative, positive and optimistic manner. This will guarantee that you'll know that you've done the best that you can without resorting to force, manipulation or lawyers.

(These are last resorts, and usually cost everybody, – okay?)

If you want relationships that are based on mutual respect and trust these will work for you.

Whenever you tell someone what they're "not doing" "not being" "not giving," you put them on the defensive and set them up to resist your needs. These are *accusations of guilt* as opposed to requests for change. Even if the other party is guilty, and admits to their faults, it's unlikely that they will be very motivated for change. Examples of this are sentences that begin with *"YOU"* followed immediately by *DON'T, as in...*

You: – **don't listen**...You – **don't care**...You – **don't pay attention**...You – **don't appreciate**...You – **don't love me**.

These are declarative sentences, – directions and commands. Think about what you're **really** *telling the other person to do.*

Absolute nots include* YOU *with the words* ALWAYS *and* NEVER *and exclude the possibility of change.

You – NEVER STOP NAGGING... You – NEVER CONSIDER

ME...
  You – ALWAYS COME HOME LATE... You – ALWAYS
SCREW UP

3)Using fuzzy and abstract words. As much as we toss around
words like love, trust, caring, appreciation and so on, they mean
DIFFERENT THINGS to DIFFERENT PEOPLE at DIFFERENT
TIMES. So, if you want some one to love you pay attention, care
about you, appreciate you, etc., you also have to get more concrete.
Tell them HOW to be these things. When you go to a restaurant, you
don't tell the waiter to bring some food. You put in a specific order...

To help someone untie him or herself we need to discard the
cards of blame and pick up on the positive.

Example   Alternative Affirmation-Concrete Behavior

You – DON'T LISTEN...
vs.
I really appreciate it when you listen.
I know you're listening when you_____

You – DON'T CARE...
vs.
It feels good when you show your caring.
I know you care about me when you_____

You – DON'T PAY ATTENTION...
vs.
I love it when you notice that_____
I know you're paying attention when you_____

You – DON'T APPRECIATE...
vs.
I need your support and validation here.

I know you appreciate me when you_____

You – NEVER STOP NAGGING!
vs.
It makes me feel good when you trust me to get
things done without having to remind me.

You ALWAYS COME HOME LATE...
vs.
I miss you and really like it when you're on
time.

You ALWAYS SCREW UP!
vs.
I'm sorry it didn't work out. I know you can do better next time.

You DON'T LOVE ME!
vs.
One way you could be loving to me right now is_____

What does it mean to be "GOOD ENOUGH?"

What does it mean to know that you are COMPE-TENT?

The paradox is you can only get to the place of certainty by admitting your ignorance.

This IS the basic part of learning how to learn. If you've stopped learning, you're dead.

Chapter 6: Becoming Competent

We all want to become masters of our own destiny.

This goal is a good one, well worth trying to achieve. More often than not, we look for an outside symbol to validate our accomplishments. If we seek intellectual prowess, we attempt to get high grades. If we want to be renowned for athletic skill, we try to win the trophy. If we are artistically motivated, a Pulitzer, Grammy or Oscar will do. Some of us do anything to obtain these rewards, – just as some of us will do anything to avoid any recognition at all. There are those of us who display our medals with pride while others keep them boxed in some dark closet.

Our problems here come from confusing what is in our power to *make* and what we need to simply *allow*. All of us have some aspect of ourselves that is a talent. We must first allow ourselves to discover what it is, and then make ourselves practice. It's difficult estimating the price we have to pay for our efforts. Unfortunately, some often give up playing to protect ourselves from failure. Others clothe themselves in the fabrics of names and titles and awards, pretending that is all they have to do in life. Since they gave at the office, or on the playing field, or at the piano, or on the canvass, they are now exempt from any other dues.

To become a master of anything involves more than being rewarded from an outside source. It means rewarding yourself for being in a *process*...

and that *the means is as important as the end, and are ends in and of themselves*. Some of the greatest athletes, composers, artists, and intellects of all time went unrecognized until their deaths.

(Don't get me wrong here, getting awards and achieving results is nothing to sneeze at either).

All of us have had anxiety about tests and performances. There are guides here that will show you how to use that energy. Most of us have felt a need to prove ourselves, and we'll touch on that. You'll get some new perspectives on being a pro, and on how being lost and exploring may be closer to each other than you think. Being the best that you can be is a noble goal, and here you may learn a trick or three about what that really means from a knight and a cloud. You can also discover how to suit yourself.

If a competent adult is anything at all, it's someone who makes choices of substance over form...

A Real Man

A real man would be able to survive in the desert for three days with just a knife and a canteen. So he thought. He read real man magazines. He worked out to keep in shape. But something was missing.

He wasn't quite sure if he was a "real man." He was employed in a nice grown-up job. He paid his bills. He voted, he made love with the occasional girlfriend; he played racquetball. He had a motorcycle, and he had some money in the bank. But something was missing.

He wasn't sure if he was a real man. So he read his magazines and books about desert plants and animals and planned his right of passage. One day, he drove to the desert, parked his car, and began to walk. He had a canteen and a knife. He had made a promise to himself not to use the precious water. A real man would be able to find water. He saw the desert stretch out before him like a woman sensually inviting a caress. He knew he could take what he wanted from her. He would open all of her secret places.

The first day wasn't too bad. The sun was hot, but not too hot for a real man. The sand and scrub pulled at his boots and slowed his pace. He had yet to see the promised flora and fauna that would nourish him. His sweat evaporated leaving a salty residue that chaffed his armpits and groin. The day began to darken into the night. The colors of the sunset danced in fire with clouds taking on the tinge of blood. They reminded him of the tissue he used when he cut himself shaving. That night he almost froze to death. He had to bury himself in the sand. His fingernails were broken and jagged.

When he woke up in the morning he had a rash that itched in all the places you don't want to be seen scratching. He was dehydrated and hungry. For breakfast he spied a cockroach. He wondered about whether a real man would eat a cockroach.

Only if he had to. He decided he didn't have to go there... yet. He absent-mindedly reached for his canteen and then berated himself. A real man could find his own water. His bones popped, cracked, and snapped him to his feet. He had some vague thoughts about a bowl of cereal. He began to become grateful for the gradual warmth that the sun's rays gave him. He stretched and began to move again.

The day took on all of the aspects of a furnace. The wind became a blow dryer. His clothing continued to soak him and he reciprocated by continuing to perspire. The walking became a blur and he could hear himself panting. The animals and plants promised in his research did not appear. Perhaps the holes in the ozone killed them off...Maybe other travelers had already scavenged the meager harvest of the area.

His footsteps became a monotony of shuffling through the now hostile terrain. He began to imagine that if this desert was a woman, she was most certainly a bitch. The thought was more typical than he realized. He categorized most women into bitches if they didn't come across with what he wanted. It had always been take or be taken with him. Real man style. (But, then again, he wasn't really sure if he was a real man).

With the sky beginning to darken, he leaned against the shelter of a dune. There was nothing to burn for warmth. He dug himself a womb into the earth, and began to shiver.

He didn't sleep that night. Instead, he fought himself. For the water. He still hadn't taken a sip. Nor had he found any cactus, or weeds, or anything. By morning he was half delirious. He remembered, right at sunrise, what happened. He saw that his left hand moved all by itself, turning the cap of the canteen. He was watching all of this as if from some distant place. In his mind he began to protest, "A real man would... ."

Then he heard another voice, from under the layers of pretense and posturing. The voice said, "Only boys have to prove they are men; a real man has nothing to prove." So he swallowed just the right amount of what he needed. Spit out what he didn't.

And came home.

Anxiety and fear can burn our dreams away as well as flame our growth...

Guidelines to Fear and Anxiety

1. Fear is a feeling that prepares us to deal with an external threat or danger. Fear deals with what we sense outside and around us. As our senses are fallible, we can be afraid of the harmless, as well as ignorant of the harmful.

2. Anxiety is a feeling that signals the potential emergence of internal feelings/desires/thoughts/fantasies that are threatening and

dangerous to who *we think we are* and who *we think we should be*. Anxiety prepares us to deal with the unwanted stuff inside of ourselves that we dread.

3. Although we may feel "bad" being afraid and/or anxious, these feelings states are both necessary and appropriate. We need to accept these feeling states for what they are, -energy that needs to be focused into action.

4. Both fear and anxiety are transitory states. They set us up to make a transition from one kind of behavior to another. They signal us to shift gears.

5. We can become "stuck" in our fear if we are unwilling to accept it as human and take action in regard to the external threat or danger. We can become "stuck" in our anxiety if we are unwilling to accept it as human and take action in regard to our own internal beliefs and desires.

6. When we feel afraid or anxious, our breathing gets restricted to prepare us for "flight or fight." (One way to calm ourselves here is by making our exhalations of breath twice as long as our inhalations).

7. Other initial actions we can take can involve extreme caution, alertness, and discretion in our exploration of what we perceive as a danger. This takes whatever time is required to fully assess the threat. It may be in the blink of an eye; it may require minutes or hours. Living in continual fear will destroy our freedom. There are no choices to be made when your security is in constant jeopardy.

8. The secondary actions that we may need to take involve the active expression of our own aggression (we take a stand and fight), or vulnerability (we surrender, and give up or run like hell), or other behaviors (we relax and play with it).

9. Whatever it is that we fear is most likely related to here and now and the future outcome of events. Whatever it is that is making us anxious has already happened in our past. Our anxiety here relates to dire consequences we experienced in the past for expressing normal human feelings and thoughts. Or our anxiety may involve emerging memories of harmful past events. In either case we may need to explore these possibilities.

10. If we take appropriate action, our fear and anxiety transform into excitement. Use it.

The difference between being lost and exploring is all a matter of self direction...

Lost and Found

The difference between exploring and being lost is a matter of uncertainty. The territory that the one is exploring, and that the other is lost in is... the Same Unknown. It had not been mapped or charted.

The Explorer expected to be in the unknown. The explorer expected to be unprepared. The Explorer expected to see the sights previously unseen, to hear the sounds previously unheard. The Explorer expects to be away from the comforts of home. Because the Explorer *knew* that *they would not know*, he or she brought supplies that would provide as much security as possible. The Explorer expects that the territory will contain elements of beauty and danger. The Explorer is looking forward to the journey while paying close attention as each step is taken.

The Lost One never expected to be here. The Lost One didn't imagine he or she would ever encounter what they now see and hear. The Lost One expected to be safe and secure in the comforts of a consistent routine. The Lost One woke up and found themselves in this strange place. The Lost One is looking backward with longing, only paying attention to anything that resembles a way home.

The very first explorers were lost. When they realized that they were lost, they decided to become explorers instead. Maybe it's more enjoyable to be excited than afraid. Perhaps if we expected to be lost we would be better prepared for the strange paths we find. Hell, we might even discover some new country. I know Chris Colombus didn't "discover" America. But, – being lost and uncertain can lead to breakthroughs and new territory. Don't knock it.

This is a story about my own ignorance and the fallibility of having to be right...

Eskimo 3.14

So one day this Eskimo walks into my office. He's wearing a fur parka. Boots. Heavy gloves. Very protected. It's one hundred degrees outside in the shade. I ask him why he has come to see a therapist. He says, "My friends are concerned about me." I ask why. He says that his friends think it's crazy to wear all of this cold weather gear in Southern California. I agree that it's a bit unusual. I ask him why he is wearing all his stuff. He responds, "To survive. All of my people wear this clothing outdoors. I have seen several members of my tribe die without this protection." I ask him what they died from. He responds, "Frostbite and hypothermia." I tell him to look at me and to see what I'm wearing. He does. I ask him how to explain the fact that I'm not suffering from the cold. "Simple," he says, "You are not an Eskimo." I have to agree with him on that one. "Besides," he continues, "I have proof that my protection is working. I have no frostbite at all." I had to give him that too. I asked him where he felt the most comfortable in his new hometown. He said at work. Hmm, I pondered, (brilliant therapist that I am). This would be the best place for him to begin the process of change. It's easier to risk where you feel the most comfortable. I ask, "As an experiment, would you be willing to take just one glove off tomorrow at work"? He looks at me as if I'm crazy, gives me a tentative yes and agrees to come back the next day after completing his assignment.

At our next session, I notice his left hand is bandaged. "What happened?"

"I did what you asked," he replies. "And see, I was right and you were wrong." Then it hit me.

"Where do you work?"

"In a freezer."

These days I let everyone wear their protections and don't initially bother trying to get them to take anything off. I figure they know the climate a hell of a lot better than I do. After I get the grand tour, well...

Only then do I fashion an opinion for another to wear.

Some of us need dragons to fight in order to justify the cost of our weapons and armor...

Hard Time Knight

He didn't live by his convictions. He lived in them. (The geography of it all almost killed him). Each and every time he became free to love, the walls locked up again. Automatic lock up. It was a very personal jail. He was doing hard time. The sentence he served trapped him in a suit of armor that magically formed whenever he got too close. The armor also changed his perceptions of reality. Where he saw his love from a distance quite clearly, the closer that love came, the more his vision became distorted. He was past blaming anyone for this. He knew that people did the best they could. He knew that he was loved to the best of their ability.

Sure, they screwed up, and he screwed up. But he was still imprisoned. He knew, from somewhere, that his sentence must have had a good reason behind it. He had learned that if you really let yourself get close to another, they would either beat on you or abandon you. In a way, the beatings were better than nothing. At least he was touched. So he walked around with armor the color of darkest night trying to find redemption. He found those people in trouble just like himself, and attempted to give them the security he once lost. He would jump on his white charger, looking to rescue his friends from harm. When everything looked happily ever after, he would take his love into his arms. Then, at his touch, his love appeared to transform into a dragon. They would commence to battle and the dragon or he would eventually retreat.

Vision is difficult when you are locked in combat. When he got far away enough so that he could really see who he was fighting, he was filled with remorse. His heart again sang with desire and warmth. Sooner or later his lovers would get tired of this trip. They'd find some other knight or prince, or even get a job. Then he would be alone.

Now, me, I got involved because I'm supposed to be a wizard at stuff like this. I work in the kingdom – it's a living. I know my job may seem like magic to some people, but it isn't. Just a combination of a lot of common sense, keeping things simple, and taking the right steps while avoiding tripping over my own two feet. Teaching our friend how to battle more effectively was simply unnecessary. He was already a warrior. Teaching him to use more restraint and to withdraw also proved useless. When he retreated, his love would pursue him. When his love found him, his vision would distort again, and all hell would break loose.

I assumed that his vision had been cursed, quite some time ago. No one cursed him on purpose. It was more the innocent bystander ricochet type of spell that got him. So we had to get him to see clearly, for his own sight was trapped in the past. He could only see what had been. He was not aware he was seeing through the lens of memory. To investigate, we examined the presence of the past. Here spells were spoken that allowed him to mirror his youth. We talked of times when giants ruled, and when forests of knees met him at face height…when his feet got lost in his fathers shoes…when ice cream was sweet and fresh and reminded him of the sound of bells. We found the truth of it all quite simply. It wasn't really a curse.

It was a Blurse, a mixed blessing/curse.

During his early years, before his armor was forged one whom he thought had loved him had stabbed our friend in the back. He had been betrayed – abandoned for another. He thought that this was because of him. (You know how self important we humans can be, believing that we are the sole cause for events in the universe). He blamed himself for this, and began to serve himself a sentence. The sentence was "I must be evil." (He had been taught the "Golden Rule." That is, if you are good, good things will happen, and if you are bad, bad things will happen. This all took place in a time where trial by combat was popular. If you lost a battle, it was supposedly because God was on the other side).

Some ideas take hold like maggots feeding on the decayed flesh of the living – (Oh, don't be so horrified. If they didn't, that flesh would rot and poison the body. Even maggots have their uses). It's just that, when we finally decide there is a better way to heal and protect, the maggots don't like to be evicted. The sentence (or Blurse) protected him in much the same way. After all, he was too young to understand that Shit Happens. You know, sometimes you get thrown a set of parents who just aren't all that capable. When you're stuck living with them for a decade or so this awareness just doesn't raise much hope or comfort. What does give hope is blaming yourself and taking on a sentence. The sentence of "I'm evil, or stupid, or cowardly, or lazy, or… ."

Then one day you can think that you might, just might, be able to convince them you are worthy enough to deserve the love. As long as you still believe, as long as you still want them to change, as long as you are still trying to prove, as long as you are still blaming yourself you are trapped. Trapped and protected, though. A true blurse, if I know my blurses. The Golden Rule still holds, you see. You can continue to allow unnecessary deprivation and hardship for yourself because… this allows hope. You must, or the Rule is wrong, which is, frankly, a terrifying proposition to any kid. Otherwise, there's no real percentage to being good except for "goodness' sake." Kids can't understand this. Percentages and fractions and stuff come later.

Good has to cause good, bad has to cause bad. Absolutely. If this doesn't work, then what's the point? You can be as good as an angel and then still be abandoned, betrayed, abused? We can't accept this as children. Most adults can't either. So we create these formulas, spells and magic sentences that trap us. All of these spells were written in runes on his armor. His armor was made of ice, and numbed him. The only way he could feel his love was when she was distant, and it was safe to take the armor off. (Of course she was too far away to touch him then, and besides, who would want to touch a maggot?) The only relief from his numbness and self-blame came when he felt his anger. At least then he knew he was alive.

He had eyes that always looked in the back of his head. If you believe that your love will eventually stab you from behind, this is a useful tool. Unfortunately, since he could no longer see what was happening right in front of him, he continually stepped on his love's toes, bumped into her and bruised her. Of course she became a dragon. This was not intentional. When she fought back, he was secure. He knew how to deal with dragons. When he began to understand exactly what had happened, and what was happening, our knight began to change. A small part came from knowing why.

Changing his convictions made of the sentences and spellings of an earlier age was the larger job. We redesigned the magical incantations and runes that were etched in the ice that enclosed him. Ice is very brittle, so you have to be careful here. It is a dance of melting a bit, freezing a bit. In the in-between where there is a softness that is a liquid , new engravings can take hold. He still kept his armor, as there were true dragons about, even in these modern times. We added hinges though, so that the armor could be removed at will.

When he first became unhinged, he had this tendency to snap the armor back into place rather quickly. He needed to do this initially, as he was also learning to master the spells that once controlled him. Each time he was open enough, we gently brushed away a few of the maggots that still clung to his wounds. He was afraid to look at what he thought would be rot and decay from all his years of imprisonment. Then one day he ventured a glance. To his great surprise, his flesh underneath was as soft and smooth as a small child's.

And so it is to this day for him and for all of us. He keeps his armor and his new convictions to the right of him, within his reach. He didn't need to wear them on his sleeve or anchored to his back. To his left, the side of his heart – he keeps his love close enough to touch. Memory's lens he keeps in the special case where he stores such tools. He decides now whether to use it or not. His vision is unusually clear.

He knows that nobody really lives happily ever after. The castle needed new plumbing, and was actually pretty cold and drafty in the winter. His love and he took it one day at a time. Sometimes they flowed over rapids, and the waters were rough and turbulent. Sometimes there was this flowing serenity that words can never fully describe. He mounted the head of the dragon he defeated on his wall. At night he looks across the room and sees the beauty that resides in every beast. When he looks for too long, his love reaches over and breathes warm and soft into his ear, and sometimes gives him a little playful bite. Just to remind him.

For those of us who long for fame and fortune...

Once Upon a Time

Once upon a time there was a writer who wanted to compose a fable...about once upon a time. He really wanted to write something that would, in fact, be timeless. He often thought too much about these thoughts of his. He realized that you could never put something on or upon "time," anyway. Once upon a piece of paper really didn't cut it for him either. Paper cuts are nasty. But at least he tried to be creative...

He wanted this timeless piece to be honest. He wanted to express *"A Profound Truth."* Then he would be looked up to and revered. Then people would come and see him as the wise and caring person he was aspiring to be. They would take his advice and

165

direction…world peace and harmony would prevail.

As he was busy with his self-appointed task, his young son crawled into his office. He yelled at his wife to "get the brat, can't you see that I'm working…." He really felt that he had something important to share with the world. His wife respected her husband, and, although lonely, allowed him that time. He worked very hard, and it took him several years to complete his book. On the day that he finished, his wife left him, and their son was sent to prison for armed robbery. His book on human communication became a national best seller in the field of pop psychology.

He spent the rest of his life attempting to track down his wife and son, who refused to talk to him.

When I leave my office for the day I carry a certain attitude with me…

Amateur Professionals

I am a professional. People pay for my services as a psychotherapist. However, I am still only an amateur in the lives of my own family and friends. A gifted amateur perhaps – and sometimes totally inept. (Ask my wife). I have a different kind of relationship here, one that involves actively dealing with my own needs as a husband, a son, a partner, an uncle, a friend… So, sometimes I screw things up. We all do. These are roles for amateurs. I need my family and friends tell me what they think about me when it's something good. I need them to tell me the bad stuff when I ask for it. I'm *asking for it* anytime I break my own integrity or threaten another's security. Family and friends will respond to this. Sometimes with action. Sometimes with words. Sometimes with silence. (All of this depending on what can be heard most clearly).

Growth is being able to take on all the shapes we need as well as being able to discard them.

Alone, Together

Now that we're alone together, I want to tell you a story. It's okay that we are alone together, isn't it? Just you and me. I mean, there are other people about and all. Even if they are right next to you, remember. I'm talking to you.

Just to you.

Did you ever feel really good, lazy, and relaxed? Like laying in a grassy field, and your eyes just drift across the sky. Cloud watching. If you let your thoughts go, and when you let your eyes get just a little lazy you begin to see all the shapes and all the forms you could ever imagine. Right there in the clouds.

Well, I got the word (from a very reliable source, I might add) that the clouds look back. They do. Really.

Clouds have their own kind of life too, you know. So there is this cloud. The cloud is a perfect cloud. There's some darkness in it, but it also has a silver lining. Most clouds do. This cloud loves being a cloud. It did the usual thing that clouds do, hired to be the earth's water delivery-type person. A Very Important Job. You've got to be pretty special to get it. You also have to work to develop those skills you need. It's much harder than it looks. Learning to use velocity, altitudes, and navigation takes a lot of practice.

Now our friend, this particular cloud, really loved its life as a cloud. It also had time off work, and it loved to enjoy all the fun things that clouds get a chance to do. Like flying and singing with the birds; visiting secret glades and hidden pools where only clouds can reach. It would play tag with other friendly clouds, and they would race across the sky until they were out of wind. Our friend loved to fly as high as it could, sometimes risking the heights of the highest mountains. It was wonderful to fly, and float, and just hang loose. It was also wonderful to be above everyone else, to really know what was going on in the land. Our friend really wanted to be the perfect cloud, and in many ways, it was so.

The cloud decided one fateful day that it would become the most perfect cloud ever born. The best navigator, the best flyer, the best of the best. Now, with this decision, it was time to restructure its way of life. Clouds that got too close to each other often merged into one big cloud. Even if they later separated, they would be forever altered by this joining. The cloud began to avoid other clouds. It was just too dangerous to play with them. The cloud refused to fly higher because of the dangers of the emptiness of space. The perfect cloud also began to avoid the low elevations. Didn't want to risk being lost in a fog. As the months passed, the cloud also gave up paying much attention to the beauty of the land. Time was spent avoiding all the things that could taint a perfect accomplishment. It takes a lot of energy to be constantly on guard like this. The cloud became very miserable and unhappy. It seemed as though that this went on forever. The cloud was so unhappy and miserable that it didn't know what course to take. Being a perfect cloud was a tough job indeed.

One day, our cloud was drifting by a deep pool that used to be one of its favorite hangouts. Lush greenery and animals that came to quench their thirst surrounded the pool.

Hello old friend said the cloud.

Hello old friend, the pool reflected. (The pool was very good at reflecting. It's one of the things that pools do best). The cloud saw itself mirrored in the pool's depths – all the sadness, aloneness, and futility of always having to be this perfect cloud. The pool reflected some more.

What is the point in being the perfect cloud?

The cloud knew the answer. *If everyone knew I was perfect, then everyone would look up to me.*

They look up to you anyway, mirrored the pool.

If I was the perfect cloud, I would reign over all the land.

That's it!, the waters babbled back. *You would reign over all the land. But you chose another course. You have held so much inside, for so long, all by yourself. Just as you are already looked up to, it is clear to me that you have been looking down on yourself. In your quest for being perfect, you have forgotten one very important thing. You have forgotten to do the very job you were made to do. My friend, allow me to soothe and comfort you.*

The cloud saw all of these things to be true. And, as our friend began to feel this vision, a strange thing happened. The cloud began to feel itself become more solid and substantial.

It was almost like being in two places at once. At first it was frightened of this change, and tried to hold itself steady. Then, realizing that this holding on was creating even more misery, our friend let go. The cloud began to fall apart. It felt itself hurtling towards the earth at a speed faster than you could imagine. As it fell, it could also see itself floating in the sky above the pool. It began to rain.

What happened next is just the beginning. As the cloud rained on all the land, all of the land reached up to embrace it in return. The peacefulness and warmth the land's touch took away the fears. It was like a dream of a dream. In this dream, the cloud began to awaken. Part of our friend awoke as a tree by the pond. She felt her roots solid in the earth, and enjoyed stretching his branches towards the light of the sun. Her trunk and bark were strong and supple and she gracefully bowed to the winds that had brought her this awareness.

Part of our friend awoke seeing through the liquid brown eyes of a doe. There was a beauty and grace that she felt in her powerful legs and hooves. She leapt over the pond as if it were a puddle.

Part of our friend awoke feeling the sharpness of his teeth, and the world came alive to him through all the scents his keen nose could smell. The wolf felt his wildness and howled his thanks to the sky. The other animals watched him from a respectful distance.

Part of our friend awoke to the sleekness of her fur, and to the pliant strength of her body. The otter playfully slid down the banks of the pool, and laughed. Just for the fun of it all.

Part of our friend awoke in mid-flight, and screamed with an eagles cry as powerful wings bore him to the high mountains that he now dared to climb again.

Part of our friend became the grasses, which held the earth safe even as the healing rain cleansed the soil that bound him.

Part of our friend became the deep pool of water, and they embraced each other as they recognized their kinship. As they swirled and danced in the depths of this new harmony, the cloud remembered much that it knew it would soon forget. It tried to call out to all who would listen, but all who could listen could only hear the babbling of the brook, the sighing of the trees, and the scream of the eagle and the howl of the wolf.

So, that's the story of the cloud of unknowing. The next time you see a cloud, or feel one come over you, remember that there's always something more than you can think or feel. Remember all the shapes that can be. Remember all that we learn to become.

In psychology the facade we wear to show others is called "persona." Here's a few ways to address it.

Suit Yourself

All of us dress up.

There are many kinds of clothes we wear. We've got our work or school attire, our just hanging out at home rags, our Sunday best, and our See-How-Sexy-I-Am outfits. We can make ourselves look rich or poor, serious or casual, neat or sloppy, virtuous or sensual. We are told, "clothes make the man." (Well, we're told lots of things, aren't we?) If we let someone know that something "suits" us, we are informing the other that whatever is going on is acceptable. In this instance we often say, "how fitting."

I sometimes wonder if the amount of different outfits any one person has relates to the degree of freedom they are missing in their lives. The less control people feel they have over their roles and relationships, the more they can shop to acquire a "new" look. If someone can't adopt a different attitude in how they see, then they can always put on a different garment. We feel satisfied for a while, until the next time. Then we have to put on something else.

We wear clothes to both reveal and conceal. We may reveal or draw attention to what we consider our best features. We may cover up or use clothes to deflect attention from what we consider to be our worst features. We do this when we are dressing for other people, because there is some reaction that we want from them.

When we dress just for ourselves, we usually wear what is most comfortable. Some of us have learned that our own comfort doesn't really matter. We wear too much and suffer from the heat or we wear too little and suffer from the cold. Some of us always wear our garments so tight that we can barely breathe. Some of us wear them so loose that we are always getting caught on some sharp angle, or we wind up tripping over ourselves.

We also dress up in another way. As we dress our physical body in various fabrics, so we dress our self image. We clothe our self-image with the fabric of *Names*. Names are like clothes we wear to both reveal and conceal. Like some clothing, others give Names to us, or they are earned and bought. Very few of us make our own clothes these days. In fact, when we say that someone has "made a Name for themselves," we are giving that person a compliment.

Most of us are still dressed in these Names we were given as children. These Names are the underwear. The new Names we buy usually cover up those hand-me-downs. Some of the Names we have inherited are beautiful, finely crafted and woven. If you have these kinds of underwear, you may need to buy very few Name brands for yourself. Many of us have underwear that are full of holes and really need to be used as dust rags. But you know how hard it is trying to get rid of your "favorite" old whatever it is. (We never seem to have this problem with socks. Socks are doomed to disappear somewhere between the laundry basket and the dryer).

The Names we buy almost always wear out, even when we take very good care of them. You see, what we forget is that some fabrics are not as durable as others. How a Name is manufactured does have a bearing on how long it will last. How a Name is worn has an impact too.

Some of us think we can wear our Names anywhere we go and

we will be able to keep them intact. Well, try playing football in your nightgown or pajamas. Try making love with all of your football equipment on. It just doesn't work.

We need a variety of clothing to fit the variety of activities we do. We also need a variety of Names.

Our self-image can't be just one suit. It needs to be a wardrobe. We have Names that we wear when we want to look a particular way for someone, because we want a certain kind of reaction. If we wear that one outfit all the time, it's going to get frayed and eventually unravel. If we always have to call ourselves "strong," or "smart," or "pretty," or even "caring," then these Names will wear out, revealing the undergarments we didn't want anyone to see.

You know, the other Names we are hiding. These are usually "weak," "stupid," "ugly," or "selfish." – Look, we got these Names as hand-me-downs. It's amazing how durable they are, huh? Without them, we would be totally naked. They took a long time to make. Oh, we have so many reasons for keeping them on. So…we do.

Now, if you really want to change your underwear, you have to remove your outer garments first. This means that we have to take off those Names you wear outside to create the Right Impression.

(You can still keep these outer garments in the closet or drawer for later use).

I know it's a bit embarrassing. Yes, bare-assing.

But have you ever tried to remove your underwear without taking your outer clothes off first? (This may be a little easier for women with dresses. However, you still have to do some unbuttoning and hiking to get the job done).

So we find ways to avoid this task. We can keep putting clean underwear on over the old stuff.

(If we do this too often, we end up looking as if we are wearing diapers).

We can use a lot of deodorant.

The problem of our dirty laundry still remains with us in any case.

Most of us pretend that it doesn't even exist. Even as we pretend we are compelled to break our backs to get the finest outer Names time and money can buy.

-All to compensate for some cheap underwear that we refuse to acknowledge we are still wearing.

When we remove those outer Names the innermost Names will be revealed. These Names are the things that we were afraid to see about ourselves. We then view all the stains, all the holes, and all the rips and tears. When I get this way I usually want to throw something on my self immediately. I call myself "good" or "together" for allowing myself to change. Well, that's a start. But it immediately covers me up again. We also need to remember something else. I remember that these innermost Names I'm wearing were given to me as a child. I didn't really pick them out for myself.

But, I've kept them, anyway.

To most of us they are like Pandora's boxers.

If we open the box, we are afraid that all hell will break loose. It often does. When we strip ourselves down to our bare essentials, and see what we have afraid to reveal even to ourselves, all hell breaks loose.

It's about time it broke loose, too. We were connected to hell for way too long.

All of the Names you are most afraid to own are in those undergarments.

All the crap we have been afraid to flush.

All the Names we have invested with the power to shame us, to humiliate us, to guilt trip us, to reduce us to feeling helpless and inadequate.

Now, I don't know what your specific Names are. I just know what they do, for and to you.

If you have been wearing the same Names underneath for years, without exposing them to the light of day, there will be certain consistent effects.

What these Names do is chafe you, constrict you, and generally create a stink. You can get the most wonderful Names in the world to wear over all of this stuff. The most fancy, intelligent, and sophisticated garments in the world can be obtained by anyone. As a matter of fact, some of us are motivated to obtain these Names just because our underwear is so shoddy. We go out of our way to look our best because underneath we fear that our worst will be seen.

Some of us know exactly what our underwear looks like.

These people put on a set of matching outside wear just as shabby.

Both groups of people are making the same basic assumption.

All assume that they are their underwear.

These are the same people who believe the clothing sales clerks who proclaim, "It's You, Darling."

Well, it isn't you. It's just the Names you've been wearing.

So, here's the plan.

First, find a place that's warm. You don't want it so hot that you get burned, or so cold that you'll freeze. Second, begin to remove those outer Names. You can put them on hangers or fold them neatly on the chair. Unbutton or unzip carefully. Only one garment at a time. There's some useful stuff here that you may want to keep wearing later.

Third, take a real good look at your underwear.

You might see that they were made for an infant, or a child, or an adolescent, or a teenager. You might see that they were always too small or too large. You might see that it's time for a change.

So take these Names off too. Now you are naked.

The best way to get all nice and clean. For underwear, I recommend something that is soft, yet durable. Something that holds you in a comfortable way, that moves with you.

These are the Names we can begin to sew together.

It's time to Suit Yourself.

SOME QUESTIONS ON BEING COMPETENT

1. What is the difference between fear and anxiety?

2. How do you usually stop your self from resolving your anxiety?

3. What do you need to do instead?

4. How are exploring and being lost the same?

5. What are the secret names in your underwear?

6. Select five people you trust and ask them where they think you're good enough.

You don't have to believe in God as much as you need to have faith in *something* beside yourself.

As for me, I've seen, heard, and felt too much that can't be explained away through logic and rational thought.

The beauty of faith is... It doesn't depend on anything.

Chapter 7: Faith in Spirit

There are things that we both cherish and fear that have no name. We fear them because they are beyond our understanding and control.

We cherish them, as they are our last refuge of hope. We cannot see them, nor hear them, nor take their measure. Despite this, we are touched by the very thought of their potential existence.

With this potential, we can see a light that has no flame, and hear a voice that makes no sound. With their very possibility we can leap off a cliff into the darkness. Some call us mad for this, and some simply talk about our wishes to regress back to the womb. The one thing that we can all agree on is that these things have very little to do with rationality.

The fact that we can *know without thinking* offends the logic of reason.

Faith in spirit is not a trick or illusion. It is a force. We would do well to respect its power in others and ourselves. We feel in our bones that there must be *Something Else* beyond this short thread of life, beyond the neuron's diminutive spark. Some meaning beyond what we can comprehend. If we are victims of wishful thinking then be advised that these illusions create realities as genuine as any other. Nations rise and fall on matters of faith and spirit.

Individuals rise and fall in much the same way.

This closing chapter offers some ideas about the use of faith, and why there will always be more than what we think we understand. You'll find out about traveling using the Odd Angle and journey an a river. You can learn about smelling Otherwhens, meditate – and be guided to partial serenity.

There's always more beyond our perception. We never see the wind. We only see it's effect.

Odd Angles

Sometimes there are these Strange Things That Happen.

And we can always make up the *Perfectly Rational Explanation*.

For example, when I look at people, and relax my eyes, their faces change in shades of light and dark.

Sometimes I see a different person completely.

Or, the time that I touched someone and their hives and warts faded right in front of my eyes. (Yeah, it really happened).

Now, I believe in something more powerful than magic.

It's also more powerful than logic.

The irony is that it has nothing to do with power, or even with me. The irony is that it has nothing to do with anything that I can sense, or even believe.

Faith is like this.

Faith is like this invisible wind that moves us toward some distant shore. We don't control the wind. We can only catch it when it comes.

There are some times and places where the calm is like death, and the stillness leaves us stranded in our fears. Then we have to paddle.

We have to use the either/oars of our own footwork and muscle.

When we have exhausted ourselves and done our very best, we will reach the right attitude for faith. Faith moves through this other time and place.

If faith is behind us, it's fairly easy to allow ourselves to be pushed without effort toward our goal. However, if the winds are blowing directly against us, it becomes much more difficult. Most of us give up here. You can do something else. You can learn to tack.

(This is not "attack." It's more like tact. Tact involves consideration for others). Tacking involves maneuvering in a way that will help you achieve your goal. When forces seem to be against you, you can learn to both go with them and toward your destination at the same time.

But you go with it using the Odd Angle.

You open your sail and point yourself 45 degrees to the left or right of your original destination. You travel this way for a while. You'll be moving forward, but way to the left, or way to the right. When you reach a point where your original destination is now 45 degrees to the other side, (instead of directly in front of you), you turn yourself toward your goal again. Keep zigzagging until the winds change. Or, until you arrive at your goal. Think of how a pendulum swings from one side all the way to the other side. It keeps going back and forth until it eventually reaches that point of rest in the middle.

You've got to be really careful when you make your turn, as it's easy to flounder here. And by the way, you may have to duck when your sail swings over the deck as your course shifts. You've got to get ready, and know that you will be off balance for a brief time. If you don't duck, the boom will smack you in the head as the sail swings towards the new angle.

If faith is the wind, then we do need a sail to catch it.

The sail is the woven canvas of our dreams that are fixed to the mast of our senses. Our sense of direction needs to be tempered by what is going on outside of us. We don't sail in storms, and when there is no wind at all, we can row. Sometimes we need to turn aside our dreams.

It is not a matter of giving up, it's acknowledging it's time to use the oars.

The either/or puts things into black or white, good or bad, right or wrong.

If the distance we are traveling is very short, and we are carrying very little, we can reach our goal directly by making ourselves. No side routes or odd angles are necessary. We just do the solid, hard work, using all our own strength and determination.

If our goal is distant, and our task is large, then we must use all the other resources that are available. Here we may need to store the oars and unfurl the sails. Dreams that just lay in storage are not very useful. When our sails are up, we must use them in all the ways that are tactful. Sometimes a direct course will work. At most other times we're going to have to zigzag. It is necessary to know which way the wind is blowing. Your mast and boom are the senses that must hold your dreams taut. Otherwise, they just flap around and cannot catch the forces we require to help us. We need to have results as much as we have a process. Our senses extend our capability for being touched by the world.

Winds that are too strong can rip your dreams apart, or overwhelm your senses so that they snap and splinter into fragments. On these occasions, we put our dreams away, put our anchors down, point ourselves in the direction of the onslaught, and ride it out.

We use the rudder of our will to make the choices of the turnings and direction we must take. There will be frequent adjustments to our course.

We cannot always see our destination. Our vision is limited to the horizon where the sky touches the earth. Some of you who have never really traveled may think that this is where the world ends. As you venture forth you will discover that there are always new horizons.

The further you travel, the more you become assured that there is something else beyond what you can see. So we learn to read the stars, and the currents, and even the movements of the clouds to help us navigate.

We remember the landmarks that have been made by other

explorers in these unfamiliar territories. We learn to use the Odd Angles.

I got a call once from some friends of a friend.

They said they had this friend who only believed in psychics.

The friend, (I'll call him "Ralph"), had some serious emotional problems, and they wanted him to see someone who could help.

These folks had heard some weird stuff about me, and wanted me to tell Ralph that I had extraordinary powers, so that he could benefit from my services. Well, I don't believe I have powers any more special than anyone else with my training and background. (I'm also not about to lie to someone, even for "their own good.") So, I told these people that I would not lie to Ralph, and that we could probably get him in to see me. I told them to have Ralph call me at the office on a particular day, without telling me what time he would call. (This was in the prehistoric times before caller ID).

When the phone rang, I picked it up on the first ring, and immediately said "Hi Ralph." It was Ralph, of course. He was amazed. Although I told him I was just as psychic as the next guy, he came in if only to find out how I pulled this off. (By the way, the other twenty-three people who called me that day were not amazed either. They were all a little confused when the first thing they heard from me was "Hi Ralph.") I apologized, and told them all that I was expecting a call. Ralph laughed when I told him how I did it. Using the Odd Angle.

Learning to think from a higher perspective means you're always right and wrong.

There's Always *Something Else*

It just goes to show you. No matter how hard you try. There's Always Something Else. It's very simple, really. Any verbal description is a linear explanation. We use words (or whatever lines we have) to re-present our reality. Much like drawing a picture, which is a two dimensional frame. Inside that frame we try to fit four dimensions. You know, the length, width, depth and movement in time. Guess what? We never get it all to fit. We never will.

Even if Da Vinci drew a picture of a ball on the wall, you wouldn't be able to throw it. When we try to put four into two, we usually end up with half. A fraction of what we started with. That is, if you are being linear. Which means that something is always being left out. Which implies that *There's Always Something Else*. Of course, what you are reading is a linear explanation in the first place. Which means that there must be something that I have left out in my description. And, – even as I've described that there is something missing, what's missing is more than the fact that I know that There's Always Something Else. Each time I try to describe the *Something Else*, I'll still be trying to cram those four into two. Ad infinitum. Which just goes to show you, – *There's Always Something Else* (Unless you include Infinity. And you can't. Because infinity includes you). So, for all of you who believe that God is dead, that things are just as they appear to be, that There Is Nothing Else… You people can cram this piece of linear explanation into a wastebasket. A wastebasket is three-dimensional. This will be a step in the right direction for you guys.

There is a reason for peak experiences. And a reason for getting your feet back on the ground.

The River

I was down at the river the other day. I thought I knew what the river was. A body of water, stretching upstream and downstream. I touch the water with my fingers, and I can feel the push of the flowing current, wetness and cold. I touch the water with my ears and hear a babbling of voices shushing the sharp angles and corners of earth into smoothness and curves. I touch the river with my eyes, and see liquid blue, the quick darting of fish between gently waving anchors of green; brownstone laced with curtains of foam. I touch the water with tongue and nose tasting coolness that quenched and filled. I smell the clean of spring rain mixed with the richness of dirt.

I think I know what the river is.

But I've always wanted to see more. I've wanted to see it all, the ending and middle and beginning. So I climb up this place I know to get a broader view. It takes some time, but looking back often takes some distance to accomplish.

And now I think I can see much better.

I see this ribbon of blue that wrapped across the presence of the land.

It begins with what appears to be a small pond. It ends with an ocean.

The borders of the ribbon are green with vegetation. I can see small specks flying through the trees. I see squares and rectangles that could be farmland, and crops, and miniature animals, and little tiny people.

And as I see more, I realize that I am unable to touch the river in all of the other ways I once could. I knew that I still don't know what the river really is.

So I go to a different place. It's neither here nor there. It's neither now or then. It's in-between all of that connecting without being connected.

It's more feeling than thought, more a sensing dream.

In this place I feel clouds bringing the rain, and sun dancing on water.

The water becomes lighter than the air. The wind carries the clouds to the land and the land funnels them back to the river in myriad ways. In this place I know that the river is... the water and the earth and the plants and the animals and the people and the ocean and the clouds and the rain and the wind and the sun. In this place I am the river too. There are no beginnings or endings, or starts and finishes. Nothing is closed off. There is this flowing and blending. Just this continual flowing. There are no limits to this. Just on and on. I touch everything, because everything is a part of me. Each particle of matter is my bed, and energy my stream. I know everything there was to know. I am the beginning middle and end. There are no secrets. It is all at once, and once is always. There is nothing to do as I am already doing everything. I am even you.

And anything else you can imagine, – *Iamwaswillbe.* There is nothing new. There is nothing different. I have done it all before, and will do so again. So, I let myself fall asleep. Not sleep as you call it. You would call it waking up. I yawned, opened my eyes, and stretched my muscles. I am down by the river. I thought I knew what the river was. Then, on a whim, I pick up a stone and moved it three inches to the left. Unseen by me, the river change its course. Five miles south the river flows in a new direction. Flowers downstream open their petals and we all blossom.

This may explain why thoughts are not the only way we know- and how the process of thought is a dualistic reaction of "either/ or."

Smelling the Vision of Otherwhens

Chaos…

When you think of chaos, you may picture some form of disorder, or entropy, or just some plain *Mess.*

Randomness, as in a "haphazard course; a lack of definite purpose."

Einstein once said that God does not play dice with the universe. What he meant was that there is really no such thing as a random chaotic event. His search for the unified field theory in physics was an attempt to prove this. He was saying that everything is connected, and that we can create mathematical formulas that would represent this unity.

He failed to come up with a valid and reliable proof.

Well, we're still trying. We are still trying to prove with thoughts what we feel in our guts and imagine with our intuition. We could also try to make apple juice from oranges.

Words and math are similar in their operations.

Both require linear (step by step or sequential) procedures to define an intended meaning. Symbols and emotions operate in a nonlinear mode. Relationships in this nonlinear mode give meaning all at once. Words and thoughts only make "sense" when there is a specific sequence of *subject-action-object*. This form of perception *implies causality*, as our use of language creates the illusion that all of reality is things acting on other things in a specific order. Our attempts to categorize, label, and to structure our world are all effected by this covert process.

The tools we use (words and thoughts) end up shaping our perceptions.

Our picture of the universe and all of our relationships become filtered through this type of conscious awareness.

We need to use other ways of understanding, without throwing out linearity and sequence. This other understanding, this other knowing comes from our hearts and dreams. Our hearts and dreams come from this knowing, as they are the one and the same.

This wholistic understanding implies that all different *THENS* exist in one *"Now,"* that our past, present and future impact this moment. We usually don't think of stuff like this, or at least, we don't think in these terms. Maybe because we can't think of two "conflicting" thoughts at once. Thinking works in a linear sequence. Why? One explanation is that thinking really smells, and thoughts and words represent the context of space. According to biologists, thinking evolved from the olfactory system, (that's smelling for us laymen) and is modified through our interaction with the environment.

Thoughts are really ways to determine *How Things Stink*.

Food, sex, danger, fear, family, strangers, – all of these aspects of our environment have there own unique smells. Smelling is a process of molecular interaction. Microscopic particles travel through the air, and react with sensory cells to give us information. Molecules have a certain structure, and we have built-in programs for those structures that trigger basic arousal reactions.

We automatically salivate, want to throw up, get turned on, develop anxiety, get aggressive, and so on.

Thoughts and words make us act the same way.

We assume that because of what someone SAYS, we have to run, or fight, or that we are with someone who is "family," or "enemy," that we are hated, or loved.

When someone says some "thing" (if they "stink" a certain way) it means one "thing." Our receptor cells and sensory neurons are constructed along these lines. One molecule "means" one thing, and one thing only to a receptor cell.

-Of course we get confused when the rest of our non-cortical and nonlinear senses give us a different message.

What if we use these other aspects of ourselves to make sense of the world? There are different places/events/reasons/causes all existing at one moment. Well, here's something crazy to think about. If *Everywhen* can exist in one *now*, can *Everywhere* exist in one *here*? Perhaps, you can see this, if you use your imagination. It has to do with what we call the space-time continuum. Our thoughts of order and structure allow us to appear to separate from this Everything-As-One. The separation is a necessary illusion. It allows us to "walk away" from the one place to eventually discover and re-create. This illusion is a cortical function. Derived from smelling stuff. The function of the hallucination is that it makes us perceive ourselves as Separate. Distinct. Apart. Excluded from...

Everything-As-One.

Here's where we get into Time. Now and Everywhen. On this hand, consider vision. Vision does not work on a molecular basis. We do not see "things." Thoughts translate what we see as discrete structures. This is why many of us can see the forest, others can see the tree, and a few can see both at once.

Our eyes interact with photons. Photons are a subatomic process. We do not see because something is "there" to be seen.

We see as light (photons) interacting with a "space," and a quantity of this light is "bounced" off this space and hits our retina at 180,000 miles per second. We do not see "things." We see energy.

Our thoughts and words make a "Thing" from this reflected

energy.

The interesting part of this stuff to me is that photons "act" as *both* particles and waves. Whether a photon of light "acts" as a particle or wave depends on the expectations of whoever is observing.

Light is both a thing, in it's own right, and a manifestation of whatever touches it. Sort of like you and me. I am an *I* and a *We*. If there is nothing to reflect the light, you can't see it. When I am just "being," "I" am not conscious of control, or structure, or form. When I am allowing "myself" to flow, or allow, or accept, "I" am busy being my actions. However, when we do "see," light appears to take the shape of what it is reflecting. When I am attempting to order, or structure, or discipline myself, "I" take on a role that is a reflection of this task. In this way, my sense of self becomes a "space," just as light appears to become the object that it is reflecting.

We experience time through our capability to visualize. We have a "memory" of our past. A picture. We imagine our future. Another picture.

Every picture can be described in infinite detail. When we speak about time, we use certain descriptions that limit our understanding. We confuse time with space. Time is "short," or "long." No. These are reflections of objects. – Or we say time is hard, or intense, or easy. No again.

Here we are describing time as a reflection of our feelings in a physical space. We "felt" hard, intense, easy or whatever.

The moment we even ask, "what is time?" we contaminate the concept of time with reflections of structure and order that are our own physical and mental attributes.

More accurate descriptions of time involve the concept of motion and movement. Time, if it "does" anything at all, passes.

Or, perhaps even more accurately, time provides an opportunity for the transformation of matter and energy. The passage of time is the movement of some form of energy from one point in space to another. In time a seed "becomes" a plant, a flower, a fruit, ... a new seed. This seed may be an apple seed; it may be the germ of an idea.

Time is not made up of anything. It has no one form, or shape, or structure. You can't hold it, or see it, or smell it, or hear it. As space is every "where," time is every "when."

Time is a very subjective trip.

You go to sleep, and hours pass that seem like seconds. You wait in a dentist's office for five minutes, and it seems like hours. So, I'll tell you the weird thing that I believe about time and us. I'll have to muck it up with words. Just imagine.

All possibilities, all potentials, all could be's and could have been's exist in one Here. Yep, they do. Just like the sky at night, with starlight concurrently arriving from both eight minutes and a billion years ago. It strains the brain to think about it. I assume that's why seeing is believing for most of us. Our thoughts don't make sense, – they make logic.

In this Space I'm trying to show you that all of the different Thens can exist in one internal Here. That "here" is not just your imagination. Your imagination is a reflection of these infinite probabilities. In some when, all those risks you never took were taken by you.

In some when, all those choices you made were different.

As awareness of the spatial field is amplified through our linear intellect, so awareness of the field of time is amplified through our intuition, or imagination. This means that, at times, we can "see" the future.

The difficulty is, we can't be sure which future we perceive, as all are possible. Every choice we make has the potential to create a new future and a new world. Information about what is and what could be does not necessarily change anything. It's how we use that information that matters. In my work with people, I trust my intuition just as much as I trust my thinking. I also know that both ways of perceiving can be misleading.

It is easy to be mislead when you are greedy, or egotistical, or hurt, or starving for some need. When I myself am hungry, and refuse to accept this, it is quite easy to think that the other smells of hunger.

Some of us get stuck in some desolate places. Our car breaks down, and we get physically stranded in some desert, or blizzard. Some of us get stuck in a *somewhen* of deprivation, or loss. Here we keep seeing ourselves abandoned, or shamed, or guilty, or incompetent. Or perhaps we are stuck in a *somewhen* of total gratification. We may visualize ourselves as some great leader, lover, or hero. Visiting these otherwhens may be useful. Moving there as a permanent resident is questionable.

I imagine there are *somewhens* where we have marvelous powers and capabilities. Where we are and have all of the things that we could ever imagine wanting. Any Utopia is dangerous. It's dangerous because it can lead to stagnation. Conflict is a prerequisite for growth and evolution.

When all of my needs are fulfilled after Thanksgiving dinner, the best I can do is sit around and belch.

I also imagine that there are *somewhens* where we are totally helpless and incapable. Where the most that we can achieve is survival. This is the opposing dialectic, the opposite extreme. There is much danger here, too. Perhaps more easily recognizable.

If I am starving to death, I may also not be able to find the energy to move. So, in one when, there is hope, which we perceive as healthy. In the other when there is despair, which we usually perceive as unhealthy. Hope allows us to continue, despair allows us to withdraw. Both are necessary.

Sometimes we need to isolate and give up the hope we have used to hold on to some omnipotent dream. Sometimes we need to join with others and give up our despair. I hope we can end starvation in the world.

I sure as hell would be upset if we ended hunger.

On a physical level, Chaos theory indicates that the motion of a butterfly's wings in China (under certain conditions,) can "create" a hurricane in Nebraska. There are patterns of interaction that are beyond our linear capability to grasp. But there are patterns and relationships that exist in all of the mess and disorder. Which means that disorder itself is our own human hallucination. To be able to perceive a new way of relating means that we may need to walk away from the desire we have for gratification and for instant results. This is the process of detachment. Mystics, ascetics, and holy men of the ages have discovered wisdom in this manner. However, they were concurrently attached to the process of being detached. (We cannot be detached without being attached).

First we may have to walk away from the physical and material. This includes the roles and the certainty of our intellect.

With this we gain access to the vision of all that could be.

Every new discovery here we may take for The Answer.

Don't worry. It isn't. It's just an Otherwhen.

We may eventually need to walk away from that as well. Seeing what could be is not enough. So we have good vision, so what?

To apply these discoveries we have to come back to here and now with what we have learned. We have to give up the vision and re-present it in the way that can fit the canvass of this place at this moment. We must detach to gain our vision, but we must also detach from our vision to touch our brush with colors to improve the art of life. Smelling the visions of Otherwhen is one way I know to come up with new pictures.

Hey, – by now you probably figured that I absolutely don't recommend absolutes...

Guidelines for Partial Serenity

1. Whenever you think that you've finally got your shit together, bear in mind that carrying around a big ball of shit can stink up any living room you enter. Being "together" is never an end result; *it's always a life-long process.*

2. The grass will be greener on the other side of the fence if they water their lawn better than you do. – Or maybe they've found a good place to dispose of that big ball of shit you're still carrying around.

Check into improving your own gardening skills prior to abrupt moves and hostile takeovers.

3. We need our walls to make us secure. We need our openings

to allow us freedom. Instead of wondering whether it's better to be open or closed, – first make a door with hinges and a lock. – Then see if it's safe to let something in or out.

4. There's a time and place for things being plain Right or Wrong. This maintains security and integrity. There's also a time and place where we really need to see things as Right or Left. This allows freedom. If we can only take right turns we end up going in circles.

5. Only fools fall in love; wise people swan dive, but they check to see how deep the water is first.

6. Since your thoughts about anything are only two-dimensional, and we live in four dimensions, it's a sure bet that most of the time we end up being only half-right. The consolation is that we are also usually only half-wrong.

7. You can't force any adult to do anything with words alone. You can provide an opportunity to influence their responses or reactions.
Instead of trying to find yourself and make everyone love you, make yourself do what you love and let yourself find others who do the same.

8. The only difference between fear and excitement is that one of them is anticipation for the future; the other is dread from the past.

9. The common factor to pity and contempt is that both require you to look down at someone. Compassion requires you to look with them.

10. There may be a good reason why Moses threw the Ten Commandments down. If your rules can't bend, they will eventually be broken, or end up breaking you.

This is one way to meditate that works for me...

Guidelines to Meditation

There are hundreds of ways to meditate, so be aware that there is no one "right" way to do this stuff. There is however, one "wrong" way, and that is *trying too hard*. A meditative state isn't something you make happen; – it's something you *allow* to happen. By-products of meditation can be an increased sense of relaxation, serenity and a deeper contact with your intuition. Visual images and colors may appear; you can feel a type of ecstasy, and a connection with *EverythingAsOneInTheUniverse*. However, the moment you try to *make* these occurrences the "goal" of meditation, you're going to mess it up. It's very much like picking a flower off it's stem to preserve it's beauty. The moment you do it begins to die. We live in this world on this planet. Visiting other planes and dimensions and communication with "higher beings" is all very well and good. If this occurs, I hope you enjoy yourself. It's always good to ask for directions, but remember your task in life is to come up with your own meaning and purpose. Vacations and escapes may seem wasteful to some. In the bigger picture, they give us energy to accomplish the goals we set for ourselves, and the ability to come back to our work recharged with new perspectives. In meditation, we need to keep in mind the goal of not having a goal for the duration of our journey. When we meditate, we are learning to just "be." We can learn to allow thoughts, feelings, imagination and senses to just "be" as well. When this is accomplished, we no longer have to be directed by reaction or illusion. We can begin to live by intent. Your Self or essence that is uniquely you is very much like water.

Now, what is the true shape of water? If we pour water into a glass, very few of us would state that the true shape of water is a cylinder.

If we pour water into a pan, very few of us would confuse the true shape of water with a square or rectangle. Our "self" is fluid in much the same way. Yes, water has a molecular configuration of hydrogen and oxygen, known as H2O. Water can also be a solid, liquid, or a vapor without losing that same molecular formation. The true form of the self can be simply formulated as "awareness." Our thoughts, feelings, senses and imagination are the containers for this Self. Most of us confuse our identity with thoughts, feelings, senses, or images that border and touch this awareness. The "I" that is truly you *is the sum total of all these integrated with intent.* In truth, our identity is based more on how we learn to interact with these receptacles of experience than anything else. The object of meditation is to get beyond the illusion of structure that traps us into being less than we really are. Here we may need to dwell on the concept of "Nothing" for a brief while. As Einstein stated, energy and matter are neither created nor destroyed, but simply transformed. The concept of zero, or nothing is a paradox. "Nothing" doesn't exist. As we explore the sub-atomic world in quantum mechanics, and the universe at large in astro-physics, we learn that there are always more particles, more matter, more energy that have always been there undetected. "Nothing" is an invention of the conscious mind. We usually consider nothing to be the absence of or negation of an object or process. In other words, the construct "nothing" acts as a wall that allows our awareness to concurrently separate from one "thing" and join with another. The object of meditation will be to remove this wall of nothing.

How we accomplish this is by allowing all of our containers, – thoughts, senses feelings and images to become equally important within the flow of our awareness. (If you've ever attempted to get everything done all at once, perhaps you've also accomplished nothing). We allow our attention to unfold in this manner *without having to do anything to or with* these emerging sensations/ thoughts. The aspect of the Self that is labeled the "unconscious" is usually monitoring and performing these functions. Our "conscious" awareness is only triggered to make contact with the internal/external world of experience when there is a "difference," or abrupt change in patterns of stimuli that the unconscious has already become accustomed to. (In this manner, a good percentage of us have learned to become habituated to noisy, smelly and God-awful environments that some other percentage of us would go mad in. To a fisherman, the stink of fish means a good day's work, to a nurse, the sight of blood means getting into emergency mode, and to a fourteen-year-old, a messy room means it's "my place.")

What we are going to do here is allow our conscious mind to engage in the same task that is usually handled by our unconscious. We are going to pay attention to the "samenesses" within our perceptual field as well as the differences. Our intent here is to simply be aware without having to do anything else. What we are doing in this process isn't necessarily rational. To make "sense" of the world is different than being able to make it logical.

So, here are your instructions:

1. Pick a standard time and place where you can be free from interruptions and other responsibilities. You can lay down flat on your back, sit in a chair or on a pillow, or do any of the more fancy positions. If you need to scratch, sniff, or sneeze at any time during this process, feel free. You have a right to be comfortable.

2. Allow your eyes to gently close.

3. Let your awareness flow to any external sounds. If you are in the city, there may be noises of traffic; in the country there may be the sounds of animals or the wind in the trees. The house or office may creak; your own breathing or stomach may make the sounds you hear. Let these noises come in and flow through you. Allow your awareness to touch all and any of these without having to take any actions.

4. Now, allow any thoughts that pop up also flow through your mind. Thoughts often come in like waves from the ocean. Some are crystal pure; others contain floating debris and garbage. Your job here is neither to fight nor surrender to these thought-waves, and to "surf" them instead, while still being in contact with external sounds. It makes no difference right now what you think you should have, could have or will do; you're meditating. Remember the aspect of your Self that is listening to these thoughts is a very different entity than the you who transmits them. As a matter of course, most thoughts here are pre-recorded commercial messages from some past authority

figure or another who is still trying to get you to buy into something that you don't need right now. You may not be able to shut the program off (just yet) but you are under no obligation to purchase.

5. While you are still aware of external sounds and internal thoughts, let your awareness contact the process of breathing. Feel the air going through your mouth and nose. Feel it going down your throat and into the lungs. Be aware of the sensations of your chest and diaphragm expanding. Be aware of a slight pause before you begin the exhalation. Let go of that breath, and as you exhale, feel the muscles relax as your chest deflates. As you breathe in, you can let your body experience a floating sensation; as you breathe out, you can relax even more. It's very much like floating on a raft in a pool or lake. You can drift weightlessly even as you feel your back and legs relaxing deeper.

6. Continue allowing your awareness to touch the sounds, thoughts, and breath, while being aware of the patterns of light behind your eyelids. Allow yourself to notice how these patterns may shift and change. At times, spherical golden, silver or colored lights may appear. Let them merge with you.

7. Even as you are letting your awareness contact and flow with these types of knowing, we also have the physical sense of touch. Hundreds of millions of sensory neurons in your skin detect gravity, temperature, air pressure, electro-magnetic radiation and texture. Permit your conscious awareness to begin experiencing these sensations. Each neuron is a part of your brain, and each has an identical structure. If you are going to learn how to use your entire mind, then remember that this is also a part of your awareness. There is nothing that you have to change here.

Start at your toes and allow your attention to wander to your instep and heels. Go up to your ankles, shins, calves and knees. Allow your awareness to contact your thighs, pelvis and buttocks. Let this continue with your attention drifting upwards to your stomach, sides and chest. Let the process continue with awareness of your shoulders, biceps, forearms, hands and fingers. Now become aware of your lower back, middle and upper back.

Allow your awareness to touch your neck, throat, jaw, chin, lips cheeks, nose, eyes, and ears. Now be aware of your forehead, temples and the back of your head.

8. Make awareness of each of these aspects of your total Self just as important to connect with during the exercise. You may, at times, get caught up in one particular "container." Thoughts, sounds, images and sensations are offshoots of awareness, just as the child is an offshoot of a parent. Avoid loving any one better or more than any other during this process. If you find yourself caught up in any one container, then go back to the awareness of your breath, and allow that flow to reconnect you with all the others. You may become aware that you're no longer thinking. (Of course you may start to "think" the moment you notice this). What is really happening is these aspects of Self are blending together, much as mixed colors create an entirely new hue. Nothing is lost here; you are integrating these separate parts to get beyond the walls that have previously trapped you. They will be reformed when you finish meditating. For those of you who are worried about "losing control," be advised that you are temporarily putting the need for control aside, while holding on to your right to gain a certain kind of power. This is the power of creativity, of relaxation and of Self-direction.

When we are no longer afraid of what we feel, or what we think, or what we imagine we truly begin to obtain autonomy. If at any time during this exercise you become frightened, then allow yourself to open your eyes or shift your physical position to regain your control.

9. Allow yourself to flow through, in, around and between all of these containers of your awareness. At one time you are hearing and thinking and seeing and breathing and touching. All-at-Once. You always have been, without the real-ization that you are doing Everything and Nothing.

The sum of this experience is merely another way to relate to yourself and the world. There are benefits to this state emotionally, physically, intellectually and spiritually. Imagine living untroubled by most thoughts and feelings. Imagine being able to respond to conflicts by responding and reacting constructively. Imagine enhancing your natural intuitive ability. Practice every day.

As you gain muscular strength you work out, so you gain these benefits as you practice. (And remember you can lift weights with such dedication that you end up screwing yourself up too, so don't make this process your god).

There is always a balance to achieve.

After a while meditating will seem the most natural thing in the world.

Because it is.

QUESTIONS

1. What and who do you have faith in?

2. If you're answer is "nothing," write about what this nothing has done to protect (and possibly trap) you.

3. Make up ten commandments for yourself and give exceptions to each one.

(Think about this...who would you like to become like?)

4. Will you make time for yourself, 20 minutes a day, – to meditate and chill out?

5. Imagine the life you'd like to have and the person you'd like to be.

6. What will you have to give up to become this?

For those of you who have found this book useless, here are a few more constructive suggestions...

Author's Note

Perhaps this book has enhanced your capability to perceive and use concepts for growth from everyday life. Perhaps it hasn't.

In any case you will discover that the book makes excellent kindling in case you need to start a warm fire.

It also doubles in a pinch to balance an uneven table leg.

It can be used to kill unwanted insects in your home.

The white spaces are good for jotting down phone numbers if you are in a hurry.

Some pages may serve to contain and dispose of used chewing gum.

If your parents are still spanking you, slip this edition in your underwear for additional protection.

Take good care,

John

John F. Elliott, MA, MFT